TRADE
IS WAR

TRADE IS WAR

The West's War Against the World

Yash Tandon

O/R

OR Books

New York · London

© 2015 Yash Tandon

Published by OR Books, New York and London
Visit our website at www.orbooks.com

First printing 2015

Cataloging-in-Publication data is available from the Library of Congress.
A catalog record for this book is available from the British Library.

ISBN 978-1-939293-81-7 paperback
ISBN 978-1-939293-82-4 e-book

This book is set in Amalia, Alternate Gothic, and Bemio.
Typeset by AarkMany Media, Chennai, India. Printed by BookMobile
in the United States and CPI Books Ltd in the United Kingdom.

TO THE MEMORY OF MATAJI—MY MOTHER

TABLE OF CONTENTS

ACKNOWLEDGMENTS

I take the publication of this book as an opportunity to acknowledge my debt to countless people who helped shape my life and thoughts but who bear no responsibility for my failures and shortcomings.

First, those who are with us now only in spirit, but whose infinite and timeless wisdom has guided and educated us through centuries—Amílcar Cabral, Buddha, Che Guevara, Christ, Dani Nabudere, Frantz Fanon, Guru Nanak, Hugo Chávez, Julius Nyerere, Kwame Nkrumah, Lenin, Mahatma Gandhi, Mao, Martin Luther King, Marx, Nelson Mandela, Prophet Muhammad, Prophet Moses, and Simón Bolívar—to mention only some among countless others.

Then, those who have joined us—in action or solidarity-to challenge the globalised trade warriors. These include—Africa Kiiza, Aileen Kwa, Aminata Traore, Arndt Hopfmann, Ali Mchumo, Amedee Darga, Benee Bunsee, Benjamin Mkapa, Dauti Kahura, Demba Dembele, Edward Oyugi, Edward Rugumayo, Fatma Alloo, Firoze Manji, Francine Mestrum, Gacheke Gachihi, Godfrey Kanyenze, Helene Bank, Horace Campbell, Issa Shivji, Jane Nalunga, Jean Ziegler, Lazare Ki-Zerbo, Mark Weisbrot, Martin Khor, Matt Meyer, Moeletsi Mbeki, Mukhisa Kitui, Nathan Irumba, Oduor Ong'wen, Peter Anyang Nyongo, Peter Lunenborg, Riaz Tayob, Samir Amin, Timothy Kondo, Xuan Li, Vandana Shiva, Vasanthan, Vikas Nath, and many more.

My publishers—Colin Robinson of OR books; Julie Duchatel of Centre Europe-Tiers Monde (CETIM), who also translated the book into French; and Walter Bgoya of Mkuki na Nyota. They pushed me all along to provide reason and evidence for my argument that 'trade is war,' and to refine my language and syntax.

To my publishing agent, friend, and advisor, Roger van Zwanenberg, I am particularly grateful; without his persistent encouragement and commitment this book would not have seen the light of day.

Last but not least, I owe my debt to my family, among them especially, Nidhi, Vivek, and Maya. As for my wife of over a half century, Mary, words of thanks do not suffice to describe your painstaking editing of several drafts of the book, but, above all, your love and infinite patience and tolerance.

PREFACE

Carlos Lopes, Executive Secretary,
United Nations Economic Commission for Africa

The narrative about the global economy has changed so much that the distinction that used to be made between international economics and development economics has become laughable. Despite many universities sticking to their old disciplines, the evidence of the change is so vast as to make the views on the economies of a particular group of countries dominating the global space irrelevant. The emergence of China as an economic superpower completely changed perceptions. Today's landscape includes many new actors from what is conveniently categorised as the Global South, clearly marking the distinction from previous times.

The new distribution of wealth and power is admitted by all. The establishment of a G20, in the aftermath of the 2008–09 global financial crisis, is a clear indication of the need to review, enlarge, and promote a new economic governance of global affairs. The G20 is a model that is based on the principle of GDP size (although with fine adjustments)—a principle that can be, and is contested but that reflects, nevertheless, the change towards a new reality. The same call has been made regarding the governance of Breton Woods's institutions, with more modest changes. It is undeniable that the Global South influence is increasing. The establishments of the BRICS as well as the Chinese New Infrastructure Bank are also significant events.

World merchandise exports have more than tripled over the last two decades and reached US$ 18 trillion in 2012, with a quarter of that trade comprising exports among developing countries—the so-called 'South-South' trade—which reached a record US$ 4.7 trillion, according to UNCTAD. In 1995, developing economies traded 42% of their exports among themselves. In 2013, they traded 57% among themselves.[1] According to the IMF, South-South trade today accounts for almost half of the total trade of China, and almost 60% of the total trade of India and Brazil. What is more relevant, the South-South trade of each of these countries will continue to outstrip their trade with the rest of the world all the way through 2050, according to IMF forecasts.

Africa is a chief example of this trend: between 2001 and 2011, total trade (exports and imports) between African and BRICS countries grew from US$ 22.9 billion to US$ 267.9 billion.[2] Although traditional trade partners such as Europe and the US remain important for Africa, Brazil, India, and China together bought a quarter of Africa's exports in 2013.[3] China is Africa's top business partner, with trade exceeding US$ 198.5 billion—compared with US-Africa trade amounting to US$ 99.8 billion in 2013.[4] India had more than US$ 70 billion of trade with Africa in 2013.

1   UNCTAD data.

2   D. Poon, 2013. South-South trade, investment and aid flows. The North-South Institute, Policy Brief. http://www.nsi-ins.ca/wp-content/uploads/2013/06/2013-South-South-Trade-Investment-and-Aid-Flows.pdf

3   China and Africa. Little to fear but fear itself. The Economist, 21 September 2013. http://www.economist.com/news/middle-east-and-africa/21586583-slowing-demand-raw-materials-will-not-derail-african-economies-little-fear

4   F. Dews, 8 facts about Chinese investments in Africa. 20 May 2014, Brookings, http://www.brookings.edu/blogs/brookings-now/posts/2014/05/8-facts-about-china-investment-in-africa

Until a few years ago, developing countries were negligible players in outward foreign direct investment (FDI) flows. Nowadays, although traditional sources of FDIs such as the US retain their dominance, some developing and BRICS countries, notably China, have moved to become large sources of FDIs. Outward FDIs from China were virtually zero in the 1980s and reached US$ 74 billion in 2011, positioning China as the largest BRICS investor.

The size of Chinese investments in Africa is hard to measure but it is estimated at US$ 40 billion in 2014.[5] China is not alone in channelling investments to Africa: large Indian private companies such as Bharti Enterprises, Essar, and Tata are quite active. Bharti Airtel bought an Africa-wide mobile phone network in 2010 for US$ 10.7 billion. Oil and Natural Gas Corp, India's biggest oil explorer, bought a 10% stake in a Mozambican offshore gas field for US$ 2.6 billion in 2013.[6]

In no other area is the Global South's growing influence as palpable as in trade. Trade patterns are a reflection of other mega trends such as demographic, technological, and climatic changes. The link between trade and growth improvements has been a subject of vast literature. Since the establishment of the WTO in 1995, the world economic output has grown from US$ 29.9 billion to US$ 74.9 billion in 2013.[7] Over the same period, global trade increased by a factor of nine, according to WTO figures. The correlation between trade liberalisation and growth has been

5   Africa and China: more than minerals. The Economist, 23 May 2013. http://www.economist.com/news/middle-east-and-africa/21574012-chinese-trade-africa-keeps-growing-fears-neocolonialism-are-overdone-more

6   India and Africa: elephants and tigers. The Economist, 26 October 2013. http://www.economist.com/news/middle-east-and-africa/21588378-chinese-businessmen-africa-get-attention-indians-are-not-far

7   World Bank data.

articulated in many studies. Even if one may dispute the exact basis for some of the findings, it is easy to admit that some countries in the Global South have vastly benefited from the enlargement of the trade plate.

All of the above being said, what agitates Yash Tandon's mind is what is lost and not achieved; What is missed and not represented; What is possible and may be halted by obstacles. For those reasons he has elected trade as the entry for profound structural transformation in global relations. He strongly believes that we live in the capitalist-imperialist era; and in this era trade is war. The concept of war in itself is complex enough to be consensually associated with a practice like trade. Tandon stimulates the discussion on trade by using provocative jibes and bullets. Even if the reader does not agree with him it is stimulating to engage.

First one needs to know Tandon to understand where he comes from. Throughout his life he has been a fighter for justice. His engagement is well known in Africa, making him a trusted advisor to leaders as much as an 'organic intellectual' for civil society organisations. Well informed, activist to the bone, Tandon is restless like the youth dominating his continent of Africa. Tandon does not have any professional references distinguishable from his political ones. He never hides his ideological positions and makes it his mark to confront other ideologies. One may not like, adopt, or even comprehend many of his positions. But as an approachable and intellectually-influenced personality nobody can use the excuse that Tandon does not engage. Not only does he engage, but he actually enjoys some controversies that allow a deeper understanding of issues.

Tandon elected trade as a culprit of Africa's economic alienation quite some time ago. He has been consistent in defending the cause of Africa's self-reliance—not the minimalist caricature of self-reliance, but rather the need to use one's own resources and capabilities to change an unjust reality. There are a lot of hopes—some could say even dreams—in Tandon's narrative. I am sure he does not mind that characterisation since he believes utopia is part of the need for mobilisation. But one has to admit his positions are grounded on analysis and study, even as one is free to agree with them or not.

Tandon's book gives a lot of importance to the historical perspective. It is true that looking at economics through history is an exercise that is always revealing and rewarding. It allows for a more informed debate. By introducing, in an almost pedagogical style, complex relations between trade and other dimensions influenced by it, Tandon proves his point about why trade is so central. That does not mean he will convince all about it being a war.

Because Africa is a region marked by trade marginalisation, representing only 3.4%[8] of 2013 global trade, it is normal for the author, proud of his African militant roots, to devote to the continent a considerable share of his attention. From my standpoint this is one more manifestation of the engagement to which Tandon has accustomed all his friends, to which I belong. The reception of his book will certainly be vast, given his known candor on these themes.

Tandon is vocal. At a time of uncertainty, voices like his need to be heard.

---

8   UNCTAD data. CL views expressed are personal.

FOREWORD

THE ABYSMAL HYPOCRISY OF THE WEST

Jean Ziegler, United Nations Special Rapporteur on the Right to Food, 2000–2008; and author of "The Empire of Shame" (2005)

Edgar Morin notes: "The domination of the West is the worst in human history, in its duration and in its planetary extension."[1]

In this magnificent book, Yash Tandon analyzes one of the main armaments used by the Western powers to exploit and maintain in bondage the peoples of the southern hemisphere, especially those of Africa: the weapon of international trade.

With brilliant intelligence, nourished by rich personal experience (as a negotiator at the WTO for his own country, Uganda, and then for Kenya and Tanzania, and as a leader of international civil society in his capacity as director of the prestigious South Center in Geneva), Tandon examines the resistance struggles by countries of the Global South around various aspects of world trade.

Take, for instance, Tandon's examination of the 76 ACP (Africa, Caribbean and Pacific) countries. All former colonies of one or another European power, these countries have long enjoyed a special trade status, in particular by virtue of the Lomé Conventions I, II and III and the Cotonou Agreement.

---

1 Edgar Morin, *Vers l'abîme?* Paris: Ed. L'Herne, 2007, p. 117.

The year 2007 saw a brutal change in European policy: the Union canceled all the preceding agreements and attempted to impose on the ACP countries conventions called "Economic Partnership Agreements" (EPAs). These EPAs are agreements that impose unrestricted free trade, liquidating all domestic market protection in the ACP countries.

For these countries, the situation is serious. The gross national product of the 28 European Union member states surpasses $18 trillion. On the other end of the spectrum, 50 of 76 ACP countries are among the poorest countries of the world. 35% of the African population is seriously and permanently undernourished. In 2014, the 54 African states had to import $24 billion worth of food. Owing to a lack of investment (in fertiliser, irrigation, seeds etc.), food-producing agriculture in many of these countries is in ruins.

Depriving an ACP country of its customs duties amounts to reducing it to vassal status, to dereliction.

Brussels' "negotiating" technique in pursuit of its goals is tantamount to blackmail: either you sign or the economic aid you receive—particularly from the European Development Fund—will be cut off.

Up until now, the Eurocrats' strategy has failed, at least in part. Yash Tandon's formidable negotiating and analytical talent, backed by force of conviction, countered the pressure and exposed to the light of day Brussels' cynical blackmail.

Antonio Gramsci was an exemplary revolutionary and an influential philosopher. He spent the last ten years of his short life in the prisons of Mussolini's fascist dictatorship. Arrested in 1926, he died shortly after his release in 1937. In his *Quaderni del carcere* (*Prison Notebooks*), he developed, with great finesse and drawing on numerous historical examples, the theory of the organic intellectual, the intellectual who, through his analyses, his visions, becomes an indispensable auxiliary of social movements.

Yash Tandon incarnates perfectly this historical function of the organic intellectual. Without him, without the power of his analytical reasoning, without his vitality, without his patience in the struggle, planetary civil society would today be far less effective . . . We owe him a debt of deep gratitude.

This book is not a utopian schema but rather a combat manual. It is a must read for all those committed to a struggle against the current cannibalistic order that dominates the world.

ABBREVIATIONS

ACP	African, Caribbean and Pacific
AoA	Agreement on Agriculture
AU	African Union
DDR	Doha Development Round
EAC	East African Community
EALA	East African Legislative Assembly
ECA	Economic Commission for Africa
EPA	Economic Partnership Agreement
EU, EC	European Union, European Commission
ISIS	Islamic State of Iraq and Syria
KSSFF	Kenya Small Scale Farmers Forum
MDGs	Millennium Development Goals
NAM	Non-Aligned Movement
NAMA	Non-agricultural market access
NATO	North Atlantic Treaty Organisation
NGO	Non-governmental organisation
NIEO	New International Economic Order
ODA	Official development assistance

OECD	Organisation for Economic Cooperation and Development
R2P	Responsibility to Protect
S & D	Special and Differential treatment under GATT/WTO
SAP	Structural adjustment programme
SDGs	Sustainable Development Goals
TIPA	Trade and Investment Partnership Agreement
TRIPs	Trade Related Intellectual Property Rights
TTIP	Transatlantic Trade and Investment Partnership
UN	United Nations
UNCTAD	United Nations Conference on Trade and Development
UNDP	United Nations Development Programme
UNFCCC	UN Framework Convention on Climate Change
WCO	World Customs Organisation
WIPO	World International Property Organisation
WTO	World Trade Organisation

1. INTRODUCTION

WHY THIS BOOK?

For the last thirty years I have been involved in trade negotiations at various levels—global, regional, and bilateral. In writing this book I draw upon written literature and official documents but also on my own experience. I attended the very first World Trade Organisation (WTO) Ministerial meeting in Singapore in 1996, and since then I have attended practically all WTO Ministerials, often officially representing my own country (Uganda) but also other countries (Kenya and Tanzania). Between 2005 and 2009 I attended the meetings as the Executive Director of the South Centre. The WTO is a veritable war machine.

I have also been directly involved for close to thirty years in the negotiations between the African, Caribbean and Pacific (ACP) countries and the European Union (EU), often as part of Uganda's delegation but also as a civil society activist.

This book is not about me. It is about the global trading system, which I describe as 'war.' If small and middle-sized countries do not 'follow the rules' as dictated by the big powers that effectively control the WTO, then they are—collectively and individually—subjected to sanctions. I take Africa for purposes of illustration in this book, but this applies to all weaker members of the so-called 'international community,' including BRICS—Brazil, Russia, India, China and South Africa. BRICS are, of course, large countries. However, in the arena of world trade, technology, intellectual property and international finance, they are still relatively weak.

My second reason for writing is to seize the narrative. Colonial narratives persist. The inequities of the global trading system are glossed over in an ideological camouflage. I have attempted to provide an alternate narrative. If you do not write your own story, you have no right to independence.

My third reason for writing is to show by on-the-ground evidence that whilst trade is war, it is not a one-sided story. Weaker nations and peoples resist and fight back. There is no reason to slide into cynicism and despair when one is seemingly overpowered by bigger forces. This book records the two sides of the 'war.'

THE WTO AS THE MAIN ARENA OF GLOBAL TRADE WAR

The WTO is essentially a conspiratorial organisation. Its decisions are made by a few select members (the big powers plus a small number of countries from the South selected by the North) in so-called 'green rooms.' These decisions are then binding even on those not present. Africa was not present in these 'green rooms' at Singapore, and yet Africa was obliged to accept the so-called 'Singapore Issues' that were agreed upon behind their backs as part of the WTO agenda. The WTO is definitely not a democratic organisation. Since 1996, Africa has been fighting to reverse the damage done at Singapore.

In 1997, following the experience of the WTO Ministerial meeting in Singapore, I did some research and I discovered to my dismay that practically all African countries had signed the Uruguay Agreements that set up the WTO without even reading the text. That shocked me. Why would they sign an agreement that harmed Africa's interests without even reading it? Why had African governments not subjected the Agreement to rigorous analysis? I also found that none of them had presented the treaty to their national parliaments for democratic scrutiny. Why not? Was it an oversight? Or was this behaviour a product of history or psychology?

I am not a psychoanalyst. But Africa's experience with the WTO reminds me of the brilliant analysis by the Martiniquean-Algerian-French psychiatrist and philosopher Frantz Fanon. In his book *Black Skin, White Masks* (1952), he applied psychoanalytic theory to explain the feelings of 'dependency' and 'inadequacy' that black people experience in a white world. Even after independence, it is difficult for black 'subjects' to eliminate the inferiority complex that is a necessary product of the colonising process. Fanon said that this was particularly the case with educated black people who want to be accepted by their white mentors. 'The Negro enslaved by his inferiority, the white man enslaved by his superiority alike behaves in accordance with a neurotic orientation.'

It sounds astonishing that, in spite of decades of struggle for independence, most African leaders have an incredulous faith in their European mentors. This reveals an implicit assumption that now that the anticolonial wars are over, Europeans may be trusted to look after African interests. Of course, this is not the only reason why they would sign agreements such as the one that created the WTO. There is the lure of 'development aid' and the threat of sanctions. There is also the all-pervasive ideology, especially after the emergence of the neoliberal economic doctrine, of free trade and state deregulation. This ideology argues that, left to the market, the resources of the world are most efficiently and productively allocated on the basis of comparative or competitive advantages. But I came to the conclusion that the reason Africa trusts Europe is, above all, the naive belief that the erstwhile colonial masters have seen the error of their past sins and can now be trusted to deal with Africa on trade matters with fairness and justice. This is what puzzled me most.

So after the WTO experience in Singapore, I set up an organisation called the Southern and Eastern African Trade Information and Negotiations Institute (SEATINI) in 1997. It has a simple and straightforward objective: to help build Africa's capacity to negotiate trade agreements; to help develop the self-confidence of African trade negotiators so they can to stand up to their erstwhile colonial masters. SEATINI has operated now for nearly two decades, and I am still its chairman. It has offices in Kampala, Nairobi, Harare, and (for a short period) Johannesburg. It is run largely by the 'labour of love' of some dedicated local 'trade experts' from Kenya, Uganda and Zimbabwe, and 'solidarity support' from some European non-governmental organisations (NGOs).

In the 1990s and 2000s, the WTO used to organise 'training' workshops for African (and other 'third world') trade negotiators to learn about the WTO 'rules of the game.' In 2004, I was invited by the WTO to lecture at one of its training sessions in Stockholm. In my presentation I made a rigorous critique of the WTO with facts and arguments. The participants were quite shocked to get a perspective on the WTO different from what they had been getting from the WTO officials and other professors. For three days, many of them would gather around me in the evenings for further discussions. By the time I left Stockholm, I had 'converted' several of the participants; they at least acknowledged that there was another viewpoint on the WTO. They began to differentiate the reality on the ground (which is what I presented) from the free-market ideology (which is what the WTO officials presented).

In January 2005 I was appointed Executive Director of the South Centre. It is an intergovernmental research and policy-oriented think tank created in 1995 by the leaders of the countries of the South. It is based in Geneva, and Julius Nyerere was its first chairman. Both the South Centre and SEATINI focus on issues related to trade negotiations, including multilateral negotiations (as in the WTO) and regional or bilateral negotiations (as in the case of, for example, Africa's negotiations with Europe). They also work on several other 'trade-related' issues, such as intellectual property, health, food security, commodities, control over natural resources, climate change, tax justice, and a whole variety of other issues. The 'mighty and powerful' countries have been able to bring within the ambit of 'trade' all kinds of issues simply by adding the phrase 'trade-related.' This is how the four Singapore issues of investment, competition, government procurement, and trade facilitation got (I would add, illegitimately) onto the WTO agenda.

Then, at the Fifth WTO Ministerial in Cancun, Mexico, in September 2003, the developing countries, led by Brazil and India, took a stand against the West`s attempt to push through a prepared text on agriculture that the West had agreed upon among themselves. Hundreds of NGO activists from the North, as well as from the South, gathered in solidarity with the countries of the South to protest against the inequities of the WTO system. I was there as an unofficial member of the Kenya delegation at the request of the Kenyan Minister of Trade and Industry, Mukhisa Kituyi (presently the Director General of the UNCTAD). He was also the only African allowed into the 'green room' negotiations. He was new to the game, but he played his cards well and managed to get three of the four 'Singapore Issues' out of the WTO agenda. The only issue that remained was that of 'trade facilitation.' Despite the utmost pressure from the Western countries and the WTO bureaucracy—led by the then Director General,

Pascal Lamy—the conference collapsed. The NGO activists danced in the conference venue and in the streets of Cancun, celebrating the triumph by the developing countries against being pushed around by the big powers. The 'mighty and powerful' and Pascal Lamy sulked after their humiliating defeat. This is not meant to be a personal offence to Lamy. In my view, he was a brilliant organiser and ideologist for the WTO.

THE EU-AFRICA TRADE WAR UNDER EPAs

The WTO experience is not unique. Europe engages in trade negotiations with Africa, and that too is an act of war. I have knowledge and personal experience (now for nearly thirty years) of the way the European Union has been pushing 'Economic Partnership Agreements' (EPAs) on African, Caribbean, and Pacific (ACP) countries. African governments, weakened by their dependence on so-called 'development aid,' are often 'willing' to sign these asymmetrical and totally unfair agreements. It could also be because of the 'inferiority complex'—the psychology that compels the 'colonised elite' to seek acceptance from their European mentors—that Fanon analysed as a by-product of the colonising process. But whilst African governments surrender to Europe, the ordinary citizens of Africa are fighting back. In 2007, for example, the Kenya Small Scale Farmers Forum (KSSFF) filed a case against their government, arguing that EPAs would put at risk the livelihoods of millions of Kenyan and East African farmers. On 30 October, 2013, the High Court of Kenya ruled in KSSFF's favour. The court directed the Kenya government to establish a mechanism for involving stakeholders (including small-scale farmers) in the ongoing EPA negotiations, and to encourage public debate on this matter. I will have more to say on this in chapter three.

A LONGER TIME PERSPECTIVE

I need to explain the use of the word 'war' in this context, and to present a balanced and nuanced analysis of my basic thesis that 'trade is war.' It is not war in the ordinary sense of the term—war with bombs and drones—but trade in the capitalist-imperial era is as lethal, and as much of a 'weapon of mass destruction,' as bombs. Trade kills people; it drives people to poverty; it creates wealth at one end and poverty at another; it enriches the powerful food corporations at the cost of marginalising poor peasants, who then become economic refugees in their own countries or who (those that are able-bodied) attempt to leave their countries to look for employment in the rich countries of the West—across the Mediterranean from Africa to Europe, across the Mexican border with the USA, across the seas from South Asia to Australia.

Of course, trade is vital for the welfare of human beings. We make things; we produce food; we provide services like banking, health, education, etc., and we need to sell what we produce. People have been trading since time immemorial. Trade does not have to be war. It can be a means to peaceful development of the world's people—it can be, and has been in past centuries. But in our times, it is not. Trade has become a weapon of war between the rich nations of the West and the rest of the world.

Slave Trade and India's Colonisation

By 'our times' I mean since the beginning of the West's colonisation of the regions of the South. For the last five hundred years, trade has been a serial war against the peoples of the South. From the slave trade to the commodities trade, it has been a story of relentless war waged by the industrialising countries against the countries that supplied slaves some five hundred years ago, and that have been supplying commodities in recent times. In the late seventeenth and early eighteenth centuries, English 'trade' with India ended up with England colonising India. The East India Company, chartered as a Company of Merchants of London trading into the East Indies, initially came to trade in commodities such as cotton, silk, dye, salt, tea and opium. Over time, by skillfully playing the game of 'divide and conquer,' the company created its own administration and military force to rule over India. The natives revolted in 1857, which the British called 'rebellion'; it was brutally crushed, and in 1858 the British Crown assumed direct control of a vast country approximately 13.5 times the size of England.

China and the Opium Wars

By this time the English had already established a monopoly on opium production and trade in India. From the mid-seventeenth century, England (along with other European countries) was also trading with China. China was more or less self-sufficient and had no particular urge to trade with Europe, but the latter needed Chinese tea, silk, porcelain, etc., for which the Chinese demanded payment in silver. England did not have enough silver to finance this trade, and so during the eighteenth century it forced China to accept opium from India instead of silver. The Chinese were not keen on opium, and this led to the so-called 'Opium Wars,' also known as the Anglo-Chinese Wars, from 1839 to 1860, eventually ending in the European colonisation of the coastal cities of China under forced unequal treaties.

Africa after the 1884–5 Berlin Carve-Up

In 1884, the European nations met in Berlin under the chairmanship of Otto von Bismarck to divide Africa among themselves, followed by cold-blooded wars against the people of Africa to conquer and reduce them to commodity colonies. They then fought two wars among themselves (1914–18 and 1939–45), joined by two other imperial nations—Japan and the United States—in order, at least in part, to re-divide the conquered world in relation to the changing balance of forces within the imperialist camp. Today, these wars continue at both levels—at the level of the collective war waged by the dominant nations against the weaker nations, and at the level of inter-imperialist rivalries.

I have abbreviated an extraordinary story. I have worked and am still working on international trade issues, as I want Africa and the peoples of the South to benefit from their work and skills. I moved from being a 'pure academic' to becoming an 'academic activist' involved in trade issues. Since leaving the South Centre in 2009, I've been invited to scores of meetings related to multilateral, regional and bilateral trade negotiations around the world—including meetings held in several countries in the South, but also in the North.

THE OTHER SIDE OF THE COIN
The West and the Rest

In this book I want to bring you up to date on issues of trade. I want to show you that the Western powers still to this day are using trade as a weapon to enrich themselves at the expense of the rest of the world. Indeed, now it is a generalised war among all trading nations. I want to show you that the history of trade, especially since the birth of capitalism, has been written in blood and violence. The dominant economic theory argues that trade is the 'motor' of growth, that it is good for nations to engage in trade. The truth is that over the last five centuries, some nations have grown at the expense of the others. Also, growth does not translate into development for all people, even in the countries that exploit other countries. It is development for the rich, crumbs for the rest. Hence, the theory that it is good for nations to engage in trade is palpably false.

WTO Paralyzed

However—and this is the other side of the coin—it is not all victory for the powerful and defeat for the weak. The outcome of war is not always one-sided. In the long march of history, the weaker peoples and nations can, and do, unite and fight back. The powerful nations develop internal contradictions within their own countries and between them, creating the possibility for weaker nations to build alliances and defeat their erstwhile colonisers. This is also happening—to some extent—in the realm of trade.

After nearly twenty years of existence, the WTO is more or less deadlocked. As mentioned earlier, several of the WTO Ministerial conferences—including at Seattle in 1999 and Cancun in 2003—simply collapsed under the weight of opposition from the countries of the South and solidarity action by the peoples and NGOs of the North. But it is an uneven struggle. At the November 2013 Ministerial meeting in Bali, the 'mighty and powerful' managed to rescue some of their issues with their 'carrot and stick' strategy. Because of their continuing weakness (on account mainly of aid dependence), African governments failed to get the 'trade facilitation' issue off the agenda (I will come to these issues in chapter two). They also made very little progress on the 'development' issues that they had fought so hard in Doha in 2001 to get on the WTO agenda. On the other hand, India put up a strong resistance against provisions that threatened to risk its grain subsidies program. Again, it is not the government of India that should take the credit for this; the glory goes to the people of India—food security is a hot issue in India's general elections. In any case, at Bali,

India managed to get an interim 'Peace Clause' that would protect its existing food stockholding program from legal challenge under the WTO for some four years.

The European Union Challenged By the East African Community

In the case of Africa, the European Commission (EC) has been using all means at its command to force the continent to sign the EPAs. As stated earlier, African governments are often willing to sign them. But the people are fighting back. In June 2010, the EC tried to get the countries of the East African Community (EAC: Kenya, Uganda, Tanzania, Rwanda and Burundi) to sign the EPAs. It had loaded it with a number of issues that the EU had lost at the WTO, such as the 'Singapore Issues.' Under a mysterious clause (called 'rendezvous clause'), it put these issues in draft agreement. There were several other clauses on the EC draft that were harmful to the economy of the EAC; the EC had fully expected the EAC governments to sign the draft at a meeting held in Dar es Salaam. On 5 June 2010 I flew to Dar es Salaam. The former president of Tanzania, Benjamin Mkapa, and I persuaded then President Kikwete of Tanzania that the draft suggested by the EAC should not be signed.

SEATINI had been working with the East African Legislative Assembly (EALA) for many years, briefing them about the risk of signing the EPAs. The EALA and SEATINI faced a major challenge. The European Commission had tied the hands of the East African trade negotiators (called 'experts'), forcing them to sign the EPA. On 7 June, the EU Trade Commissioner Karel De Gucht flew into Dar es Salaam with his team, fully expecting that the EC draft would be signed. Dar es Salaam was a battleground for three days. The East African civil society groups, among them SEATINI, were engaged in a veritable guerrilla war with the EC team, backed by elected MPs of the EALA. Four days before De Gucht flew in, on

3 June, the EALA had passed a resolution which, among other things, expressed its concern that if the outstanding issues were not resolved, 'the EPA framework will bind the EAC to poor trading terms.' By the time De Gucht came, the EC had already lost. The ministers heeded the EALA resolution instructing the Council of Ministers to 'delay signing . . . until all controversial issues were resolved.' The agreement was not signed.

A month earlier, on 13 May, 2013, SEATINI—together with twenty-two other civil society organisations—had sent a written appeal to the EALA warning it against the US-EAC Trade and Investment Partnership Agreement (TIPA) that the US had been pushing the East African Governments to sign since October 2012. TIPA is similar to the Transatlantic Trade and Investment Partnership (TTIP) that the US has been pushing European Governments to sign. TTIP, too, has produced strong voices of opposition from the EU civil society organisations.

Earlier, I gave the example of how in October of 2013 the Kenya Small Scale Farmers Forum had succeeded in getting the High Court of Kenya to stop the government from proceeding with the EPA treaty without an open debate and the full participation of all the stakeholders.

Of course this was the situation in 2014. I will deal with some of the developments that occurred subsequently in chapter three.

People as the Movers and Shakers of History

One thing is certain: history does not always move according to the wishes of privileged individuals in power. They are not always, or not only, the 'movers and shakers' of history. That is why democracy, the consent of the people, is so important. Democracy, of course, is a process, a work in progress. Even in the most democratic states, the will of the people is often hostage to the imperatives of electoral politics and the manipulation of 'special interests,' as they are called in the United States. There is simply no 'perfect democracy,' or a 'democratic model.' Claims to such must be palpably dishonest. People matter. When things are down and out for them, they take to the streets, sign petitions, organise rallies, go to jail, and mobilise the media. Activists, for their part, write petitions, produce analytical papers breaking down the technicalities of trade language for ordinary people and the media to understand, lobby ministers, and organise brainstorming and strategy meetings. And if things are really bad, people resort to armed struggle, as has been the case in many parts of Africa, Asia and Latin America during struggles against the imperial order.

WAR AND PEACE

This is what this book is about. It is about war, and it is about peace. I discuss these on the terrain of trade. Stark options face those who fight trade wars, for the consequences of victory or defeat are, or can be, catastrophic. Telling a simple narrative, however, is an insufficient objective. For the objective of this book is deeper than simply arguing that trade is war. There are moral issues that underlie trade, just as they do all other kinds of war. People talk about, for example, 'fair trade' or 'levelling the playing field,' or providing 'special and differential' trade deals for the weaker nations of the South. These are not just the bizarre whims of 'NGO do-gooders,' even if these sentiments are ignored or diluted in the rough-and-tumble of trade wars, as we shall see in the body of the book.

What guides the book, above all, is a desire to keep alive the spirit of revolutionary optimism, and not to lapse into cynicism and despair when one is seemingly overpowered by bigger forces. In the last chapter I discuss the strategy and tactics of what I dare to call 'guerrilla war against imperial peace.' If you want peace, prepare for war. I hold the view that nonviolent methods of resolving conflicts over trade are less divisive, more effective and more enduring. I philosophise a bit, though I am no philosopher. I talk about my 'philosophy of contradictions.' But I must stop here. You cannot reveal everything in a short introduction.

2. THE WTO AS AN ARENA OF GLOBAL TRADE WAR

Having participated in the deliberations of the WTO practically since its creation, I can say without hesitation that the WTO is an extended arm of US and EU trade and foreign policy. The South is united by colonial experience, but they are divided through manipulations by the imperial powers due to their internal weaknesses. However, the countries and peoples of the South can resist imperial pressures and manipulations. But that requires concerted reflection and action on their part.

INTRODUCTION

The WTO was created 1 January 1995. It was designed to benefit the United States, the European Union and Japan at the expense of the rest of the world.

My aim is to show how the West, despite the endless rhetoric about 'development,' has no interest in the development of the rest of the world and is in fact in a relentless 'war' against it. If the rest of the world develops, it is through their own persistent struggle to carve out a space for themselves—a theme I shall develop in chapter six. The West's chosen instruments of domination are aid, trade, investment, and technology. At the end of the Second Imperial War (1939–45), the victor nations (the 'Allied' powers) met at Bretton Woods in the US to create a whole new structure of global governance. Three major international bodies were created: the World Bank, the International Monetary Fund (IMF), and the General Agreement on Tariffs and Trade (GATT). Whilst the first two dealt with matters of finance and development, GATT dealt with trade regulations and agreements. In 1995 GATT was replaced by the WTO (though, formally, GATT and its rules continue to remain an integral part of the WTO system).

I need to explain Western insensitivity towards non-Western development through a brief look at history. By the end of the eighteenth century, Britain was the dominant industrial nation. By the end of the nineteenth, it was joined by others—most of what we now know as Western Europe, the United States, and Japan. The earlier empires of Portugal and Spain had declined. The Dutch empire, too, was declining, but it managed to revive itself in the wake of industrial capitalism. The other declining empires were the Ottoman and Russian empires. Russia was on the precipice of a pre-revolutionary period. The rest of the world did not count—either already colonised (like India), partially colonised (like China), neo-colonised (like Brazil), or about to be colonised (like Africa and the remnants of the Ottoman Empire).

Is this too simple a narrative? Of course it is. But the core of the matter lies in its simplicity. By the turn of the nineteenth century, while Russia was in chaos and America was busy colonising its own hinterland (like Mexico) and former Spanish colonies (like Cuba), and neo-colonising South America, the Europeans met in Berlin in 1884–85, put a map of Africa on the table and systematically divided sub-Saharan Africa among themselves. There were some 'independent' countries. Liberia was one of these, but it was already an American 'colony.' South Africa and Ethiopia were later 'conquered'—the first by the British and the second by Italy. So from the end of the nineteenth century to the end of the Second

Imperial War in 1939–45, the 'world' was comprised of the 'West' and the 'Rest.' The West ruled; the Rest did not matter.

Colonial and financial empires as practiced in the nineteenth and twentieth centuries by Europe and America were consciously designed to benefit their own peoples, not the colonised peoples. The latter were coerced through political, economic, and military domination to produce raw materials, food, and minerals that were processed in the empires.

Things changed after 1945. The colonised peoples revolted against the imperial system. Also, the US demanded that the European imperial nations open their colonies to American trade and investment. Under this double assault, Europe was obliged to 'give' the colonies political independence. However, the old systems of direct financial and trade controls were revamped into new forms to serve the same imperial objectives. This story shows how the Europeans and the Americans maintained their dominance over trade and production in the old colonies of the South. The conditions in the world changed again after 1989 with the collapse of the Soviet Union. The developed countries decided they had different needs and again altered their demands through a series of international trade treaties—but to this I shall come later.

The above is only one part of the story. The other part is the resistance by the Rest against the West. No war is totally one-sided. Things change, though they may take a long time. The West is not having it all on its terms. We now live in a different world. But to this also I shall come later.

KIGALI AND GENEVA
Kigali
In November 2011, I was a participant at the Sixth Ordinary session of the African Union Trade Ministers meeting in Kigali, Rwanda.

The Prime Minister of the host country opened the meeting by raising a poignant point: Africa's share of global trade is dropping. Why? And what do we do about it? After he left, the Rwandan Minister of Trade and Industry, Monique Nsanzabaganwa, who came in as the chair of the AU Trade Ministers conference, took over to lead the discussion. She argued that Africa must prioritise intra-Africa trade over global trade and move towards a 'borderless Africa.' Then Erastus Mwencha, Deputy Chairperson of the African Union Commission (previously, Secretary General of the Common Market for Eastern and Southern Africa—COMESA) took the podium and argued that Africa was too vulnerable to external shocks; it must reduce export dependence and regionalise. He hoped that the ongoing tripartite negotiations between COMESA, the East African Community (EAC) and the Southern African Development Community (SADC) would mature into a full-fledged free trade area in the continent. It was a sobering picture of Africa, but there was hope that Africa might do better if it was organised better.

The only discordant note from the podium came from Pascal Lamy, then Director-General of the WTO (previous to which he was *chef de cabinet* of the European Commission). Contrary to what the Africans had said, he argued that Africa had gotten past its worst economic crisis; that the continent had been enjoying 'robust growth' because of 'prudent economic policies'; and that 'trade must be at the heart of Africa's recovery and growth in order to achieve the Millennium Development Goals (MDGs).'[1] Lamy obviously had a fantasised picture of Africa to which his officials had obligingly added 'facts and figures' using conventional categories like GDP and FDIs.[2]

The rose-tinted glasses of neoliberal economics through which Lamy and international trade bureaucrats in general 'see'

Africa betrays their ideological colours. Africa is 'doing well' because it is following 'prudent economic policies,' no doubt at the behest of the IMF, the World Bank, and the WTO. These bureaucrats are so immersed in the minutiae of trade negotiations that they cannot see the forest for the trees. But even when they take their eyes off the trees of trade details, they only see the forest through the myopic vision of neoliberalism.

However, occasionally the forest becomes visible through hindsight, at least to some politicians. In October 2008, for example, Bill Clinton said at the UN that 'we all blew it, including me as president' by treating food crops as commodities rather than a right of the poor. He reprimanded the World Bank, the IMF, and other global institutions, and cited corn subsidies and US food-aid policies as key problems contributing to the global food crisis.[3] In the WTO, however, despite Clinton's lament, food remains a tradable commodity. The WTO's past follies and foibles, especially the effects of its dogged determination to push free-market fundamentalism, are visible in many parts of the world, particularly Africa.

Geneva

I have lived for most of life in Africa, except for those years when I was a student in London in the late 1950s, and then in New York as a visiting research fellow in 1967–68. I have been to other capitals of the West—including Geneva—on many occasions, usually to attend conferences and meetings. But I came to live in Geneva in the years 2004 to 2009, when I was appointed the Executive Director of the South Centre. It was for me a unique, mind-opening and often bizarre experience—exciting in some ways, daunting and intimidating in others.

Geneva has a surreal atmosphere about it. It is not really part of the 'normal' world, at least not the world of the South, where two-thirds of humanity lives. The reliable public transport system timed like a Swiss clock and the peaceful surroundings of Swiss mountains and Lake Geneva provide the cool ambience in which diplomats from the South and the North negotiate matters from trade to intellectual property regimes, from disarmament to human rights. Geneva projects a comfortable veil of (apparent) aloofness from the real world. The negotiations have an air of abstraction from the reality of power politics. The harsh and cruel realities of an often violent world out there, especially in the Global South, become distant. Geneva is a synthetic, sanitised place.

This is both good and bad. It is good because it provides a certain degree of comfortable decoupling of international trade negotiations from the messy daily life of food shortages and deaths from AIDS, Ebola, and terrorist attacks. But it has a reverse side to it. The existential detachment also leads to conceptual detachment. Thinking becomes universalised and idealised, abstracted from reality. And when it comes to trade negotiations within the sublime waterfront façade of the WTO, mathematical formalism—an abstruse numbers game—takes over in ever-repeating incantations. Coefficients and percentages parody life. This is true regardless of whether the trade negotiators are working on matters related to manufacturing and industry (curiously known by the negative formulation 'Non-Agricultural Market Access,' or 'NAMA') or on matters related to agriculture (or 'Ag,' in the expert lingo).

In this rarefied field of negotiations, metaphors ranging from 'landing grounds' to 'taking a walk in the woods' circulate from desktops, to evening party talks, to the media. Sadly, as trade negotiators take a walk in the woods, they count the trees and often lose sight of the forest. They may think they have won the numbers game, but in the process they are often unaware that they may have gotten lost in the forest.

THE WTO: AN IDEOLOGICAL AND SANCTIONS-BEARING WAR MACHINE
The WTO's Two Pillars
1. Trade liberalisation ideology flouted by history

For the last thirty years, trade liberalisation has been hyped up as the 'engine of growth' by the Washington Consensus.[4] It is one of the major tenets of the dominant neoliberal economic ideology of our times. The strange truth about this ideology is that it is, paradoxically, a total abstraction from reality. It has no real life. Its essential, underlying principle of free markets had its heyday when England ruled the seas in the nineteenth century. But as soon as the United States was ready to industrialise in the latter part of the nineteenth century, it challenged the free market ideology of the British. As it went into full-blooded industrialisation, the US put in place protectionist barriers against 'free trade.'

After the 1870s, the US example was emulated by Germany, France, Japan, Switzerland, and every other European country on the path to industrialisation. Today, neoliberal economists have resurrected it as a mantra for development, and as a way to oppose rival economic theories (such as Keynesian economics[5]) and foreclose on all state intervention in the economy. But the irony is that this 'free market' theory applies only to the countries of the South. Policymakers and academic theorists should not take this ideology seriously. I have been involved in trade negotiations for close to thirty years, and I can give ample examples (as I do later in this chapter) to show that despite their rhetoric, the countries of the North use protectionist measures, state subsidies and all the tactics of 'closed' economies. It is not only Northern governments that ensure that their economies remain closed; it is also monopolistic Northern corporations. The vacuous basis of this 'free-market' ideology was amply exposed in the financial meltdown of the casino economy since 2007–08.

2. How did sanctions get into the WTO system?

The second pillar—enforcement—needs to be critically reviewed. It is based on the premise that the negotiated texts of the WTO are binding, and so no country can ignore the WTO. In international legal parlance, this is technically true. The WTO is perhaps the only organisation (besides the Security Council of the United Nations) that has teeth. The WTO can bite. Its architecture legalises sanctions by an aggrieved party against an offender. Why the WTO was given teeth in the first place, whilst its predecessor, the GATT, had none, is a question that can be understood only with a bit of knowledge about how the WTO was created. This is not an idle question. Sanctions are an act of war (a subject more fully explored in chapter five).

So let us begin from the beginning. Where does the idea that 'the negotiated texts of the WTO are binding' come from? What does 'legal obligation' under the WTO mean? Tariff reductions, for example, are bargained exchanges under the rule of reciprocity, and yet the principle of Most Favoured Nations (MFN) contradicts this 'bargained-for reciprocity.' Let me explain. The MFN is a principle of non-discrimination between trading partners. It says that any trade advantage, privilege or immunity one state grants to another shall be accorded on like terms to all its trading partners. To give a simple example, if Uganda allows China free-market access to clothing, then it should make the same allowance for Britain. But then, how does this square with the principle that all trading deals are reciprocally bargained exchanges? This is an important issue. For example, in Africa's negotiations with the European Union, the EU insists that any deal Africa makes, for example with China, must be extended to the EU too under the MFN principle. But why should Africa, after tough bargaining with China for which presumably it gets something in return, extend the same terms to Europe? It simply does not make sense. The MFN is one of the most absurd principles of the global trading system—and there are others.

The question of how and from where the WTO gets its 'rules-based system' is a deep jurisprudential question. It is important to understand this too in order to make sense of the WTO system. But I will not go into this here. It is a complex subject.[6]

However, it is important to get into the history of the subject. And for this it is necessary to go to the arrangements made before the WTO came into existence. The WTO is a leftover of the failed attempt to create the ITO during the Bretton Woods negotiations after the Second World War. The ITO's initial enforcement proposal focused on remedies for violations in the form of *compensation* for injury rather than *sanctions*. The ITO's proposed enforcement mechanism was a three-step procedure: complaints were investigated and ruled upon by the Executive Board; rulings of the Board could be appealed to the conference consisting of all Members; and then final appeal lay with the International Court of Justice (ICJ), but only 'if the conference consents.' France and Benelux were opposed to giving the ITO the power of sanctions; they were concerned that the ITO might be politically influenced by the power of the Anglo-American dollar/sterling empires. The US and UK, on the other hand, pursued the sanctions route. They argued that mere compensation negated a 'higher moral duty to abide by promises.' The ITO never got off the ground, but (at the insistence of the Anglo-Saxon countries) the shell that was left behind—namely the WTO—incorporated in its system the language of sanctions.

THE QUESTION OF 'FAIR TRADE'
The 'Feel-Good' Effect of the Notion of Fair Trade
Sanctions and enforcement are only one challenging aspect of the WTO. One question that arises from the WTO's dispute-settling

mechanism is whether the WTO's decisions establish legal and ethical norms, and precedents, as in case law in domestic legal systems. This is another complex subject.[7] My question is slightly different. It is not about a 'positivist' or a teleological evolution of trade law. It is related more to the notion that the WTO should be guided by ethical norms; that an *ad hoc* approach to trade issues puts too much power in the hands of the powerful, who need to be made accountable to notions of fairness and justice; and that there needs to be a 'levelling of the playing field' before nations can engage in fair trade—a notion that I partly share. The notion of 'fairness' has an obvious normative appeal. It is this notion of 'fair trade' that is the basis of things like 'fair-trade' coffee or cocoa or bananas in shops in Western countries.

I support the idea of 'fair trade' as an ethical idea. Also, it is a kind of 'counter-sanctions' against the big and powerful corporations that deal in 'market' prices. Once again, the irony is that giant trading companies like Wal-Mart and Tesco have caught on to this idea; they have shelves where you can pick up 'fair-trade' coffee at a slightly higher price than 'ordinary' coffee. For consumers in the West that wish to express solidarity with poor Ethiopian or Guatemalan coffee farmers, buying 'fair-trade' coffee has a 'feel-good' effect. And that's fine. But I do not think that this even scratches the surface of the problem of what, at root, is 'unfair trade.'

Mirror, Mirror on the Wall, Who's the Fairest of Us all?[8]

The hard reality is that trade is war. In other words, to put it bluntly, the notion that 'fair trade' will lead to fair trade is an illusion, and a bit of a distraction from looking at the hard reality. Here I write as one who has been involved on diverse sides of this debate. I have walked around the sites of WTO conferences in

Singapore, Geneva, Seattle, Doha and Cancun with banners reading 'Fair Trade for Africa,' or similar invocations. But I have also sat through hard-headed negotiations where the state notion of 'fair trade' is almost diametrically opposed to the non-state (NGO) notion of 'fair trade.'

Let me illustrate the last point by taking the case of the United States. US trade law makes a distinction between two kinds of unfairness claims: offensive and defensive. Cases of 'defensive unfairness' arise when foreigners have unfair trade barriers against US exports, and 'offensive unfairness' when foreigners dump products into the US market.[9] Of course, the American notion of unfairness may not be shared by, for example, Japan, China, or India. For thirty years after the Second World War, the US rejected claims that its corporations had unfair advantages because of their size. As Japanese steel companies grew in size, the US began to claim that size gave Japanese companies an unfair advantage. In other words, the US used the 'fair trade' concept to pry open foreign markets until Japanese competition became 'unfair.'[10]

The Question of 'Standards' in the WTO's Doubletalk

There is another dimension of 'fair trade' when policymakers and NGO activists develop their defensive 'war strategy.' It is related to the notion of fairness as applied to the issue of 'standards.' The industrialised countries (ICs) of the North often argue that the developing countries (DCs) have an 'unfair advantage' over them because unlike the DCs, their producers have to meet high environmental standards in production. The DCs, supported by justice-oriented NGOS, argue that it is 'not fair' to expect the DCs to meet the high standards of the ICs when they do not have the necessary technology to reach those standards. This argument, when advanced in the context of negotiations on climate change, has been tacitly accepted by all. Under the Kyoto Protocol[11] there is an acceptance that if the ICs want the DCs to engage in 'sustainable' production, then they must provide the necessary capital and technology. Of course, the implementation of the Kyoto Protocol is quite another matter, one that continues to be deadlocked. But that is another subject.

'Will you Walk into my Parlour,' said the Spider to the Fly

Let us pause. I realise that the last few pages have been quite dense. I have tried to describe a very complex organisation in a few pages. The WTO is a veritable battleground where the warring parties fight over real issues—issues that have an immediate effect on the lives and jobs of millions—using sophisticated technical arguments, legalisms, moralisms, and ideological and political weapons with a deftness and chicanery that is hard to imagine in any other context. People have made lifetime careers working in the organisation, or in national ministries dealing with the WTO, or studying it and the international trading system. I began to understand the system (I dare say) in its complexity after closely monitoring it over almost twenty years as an NGO activist and also as someone inside the negotiating chambers of the WTO. The WTO is an intricate cobweb in which the spiders and flies 'play out' their deadly games.[12]

On the surface it all looks 'cool' and benign, but the loss of an argument here or an errant text there (or even just one wrong word) can lead to a country being subjected to 'sanctions'—a coercive measure that is legalised by the WTO enforcement system. Or it could lead to a regime of trade being imposed on it (such as a reduction in tariffs or a removal of subsidies) that could in turn lead to deindustrialisation and unemployment, as indeed has been the situation with many of the middle-sized countries and the so-called Least Developed Countries (LDCs) of the Global South, in particular in Africa.

The above account is a small part of a much larger and more complex and often convoluted debate. It is enough to give an idea of what the WTO is all about, and to introduce a minimum of WTO language (or 'double-talk'), for us to make sense of the pages that follow. In preparing for war one does not build ones strategy on illusions such as the notion of 'fair trade'; one builds them on the reality on the ground.

DOHA: 9–14 NOVEMBER 2001

Within two hours of my arrival at the Doha international airport, I was at the Conference Centre, the venue for the Fourth WTO Ministerial Conference. I was attending the meeting as head of the Southern and Eastern African Trade Information and Negotiations Institute (SEATINI), an NGO institution I had founded after the First WTO Conference in Singapore in 1997. In addition, I was also, officially, part of the Uganda delegation, and unofficially an adviser to the Head of the Tanzanian Minister of Trade and Industry, Iddi Simba. The previous year, he had invited me to participate in the conference of the Least Developing Countries (LDCs) in the historic dhow city of Zanzibar. Together with Ali Mchumo, then the Tanzanian Ambassador to Geneva, and Martin Khor, then head of the Third World Network in Geneva, I was on the committee that drafted the declaration at the end of the LDC conference. At Doha, Iddi Simba represented the interests of the LDCs; he therefore held the crucial position of spokesperson for 'the poorest nations in the world.'

There were a number of issues that united the LDCs and the developing countries generally, among them: agriculture and food security; non-Agricultural Market Access (NAMA); the Singapore issues; the perennial issue of 'special and differential' (S&D) treatment for the LDCs; and the waiver issue in relation to the negotiations between the EU and the African, Caribbean and Pacific (ACP) countries.

Here, however, I analyze the processes rather than the issues, which I address later in the chapter.

On the last day (actually, in the early hours of 13–14 November), delegates from mostly Southern countries were sitting around in the outer lounge of the main auditorium watching CNN, which was showing US bombs pounding Afghanistan. We were waiting for news on the state of the 'dreaded' text. We had heard about the 'green room' where hard negotiations were taking place. In fact I had tried, on behalf of Uganda, to enter the 'green room' and had failed. In the 'green room' the Tanzanian Minister, Iddi Simba, and Ambassador Ali Mchumo were badgered all night until the early hours of the morning to agree to the text on behalf of the LDC, or else . . . . [13] We had heard in the corridors that the US had let it be known that since 9/11 the global situation had changed: those who would 'conspire' to repeat the Seattle debacle at Doha would be aiding the 'terrorists.' The WTO meeting in Seattle in December 1999 had been a disaster. The media blamed the activist NGOs for its collapse. At odds with this 'reality,' the countries of the Global South had celebrated Seattle's demise. The US threat turned Doha into a victory for the North and a defeat for the South.

THE THREE-LAYERED REALITY OF THE WTO

Doha was declared 'successful. by the big powers and the mainstream media. Was it? That is the question I pose here. The answer must be that it depends on what level of reality one uses to evaluate the process and outcome of Doha, for there are three levels of reality: the official narrative on the surface; the reality below the surface, like shadows in a moving stream; and the philosophical-ideological-ethical reality at its deepest level.

The official narrative (propagated by the WTO, Western governments and the mainstream media) is that at Doha, a 'negotiated' document was presented on the last day, and the assembled delegates all gave their 'consent' to the declaration. There were some dissenting voices here and there, and some of these concerns were 'accommodated' at the last minute. For example, India had held out to the last day, and even threatened to withdraw its consent. The African, Caribbean and Pacific (ACP) countries wanted a waiver on the EU-ACP Agreement. However, in the closing minutes of the extended session, they withdrew their earlier objections against the draft declaration. The essential point is that 'nobody walked out of the meeting,' and at the final plenary session they all fell in line behind the document as an expression of 'the collective will of the international community.'

This is one level of reality. Its denial serves no purpose. Here, as I indicated earlier, I am looking at the process of 'negotiation,' not at the substance of the Doha Declaration. If you challenge the official narrative and try to expose the deeper layers, you face the question, why did the objecting states not withdraw their consent? Thus, no country is in a position to complain about the Doha Declaration. They all 'conceded,' and they must now bear the consequences. Even those countries that may have felt that they were pressured to sign something they did not believe in cannot say, at the formal or official level, that they were not part of the consensus, or even admit, in public, that they we pressured to sign. The Doha declaration is now a *fait accompli*. It is part of the future reality.[14]

The second reality is deeper. The US and the EU played the 'game' of trade negotiations as if they were at war with the developing countries, not very different *in spirit* from the war they were waging in Afghanistan. They exercised their muscle and they wielded their ample purse; it would be a naive observer who would want 'evidence' of this. *Things done in the dark are, by definition, invisible.* I do not have knowledge of what happened behind the scenes between the US/EU and India. But I know what was afoot on the LDC and the waiver issue. Waivers are not something extraordinary. For example, the US has been getting WTO waivers on an agreement it made with Africa called the African Growth and Opportunity Act (AGOA). If Europe wanted a waiver on its own Economic Partnership Agreement (EPA) with Africa, it would have known how to get one. But in Doha, Europe chose to make a big issue out of telling the ACP countries: sign the rest of the Declaration, or else there will be no waiver, and the ACP countries will lose their preferential market access to Europe. Small-scale banana producers from Africa and the Caribbean would then have to compete against plantation bananas from the Philippines and Ecuador. Until that moment, the 'third world' had shown remarkable unity and solidarity. Their trade experts from Geneva showed a remarkable grasp of technical issues—let no one say that they did not know what they were signing. This time they did, unlike at Uruguay in 1994, when the WTO was created, or at the First WTO Ministerial in Singapore in 1997. At the end, in Doha they had to give in. Why? Because in a war situation, the weak have to surrender what they cannot hold by the strength of their economy and political will.

The third reality is even deeper, like the bottom of an ocean. It concerns rules of 'good governance,' 'democracy,' and 'fair play.' Doha was a product of a manipulation of the rules of decision-making. Practically every single rule in the rule book on the conduct of international conferences, and specifically on the conduct of the Ministerial Meetings of the WTO, was broken from the beginning to the end. The big players made the rules as they went along. Thus, from the time the first draft statement was issued in Geneva on 26 September 2001 by Stuart Harbinson, the Chairman of the General Council, to all succeeding drafts, to the appointment of the 'Friends of the Chair' (without consultation with the General Council), and their conduct, and to the last 'green room' (I call it the 'boiler room'), the WTO Secretariat and the representatives of the big powers were 'making new rules' as and how it suited their interests. At the end of the day, if the weaker members did not have the guts, or the will power, to 'withdraw consensus' and walk out, they were like caged animals forced to accept any rule, or change of rule, until the final showdown on the last plenary.[15] The only rule that governs the WTO is that if you do not accept its rulings, you withdraw your consent. If you can't, then tough luck.

The only saving grace of the Doha Round was the addition of the word 'development.' So immediately after Doha it was called the 'Doha Development Round' (DDR). However, the Western, 'already developed' countries are trying hard to get rid of the middle word. Their governments and the media often refer to the Doha outcome as the 'Doha Round.'

Having looked at how decisions are made in the WTO—the processes—let me now turn to the substance of the trade agenda.

THE CHANGING AGENDA OF TRADE NEGOTIATIONS
From the WTO to UNCTAD and Back to the WTO

The issues that come under trade negotiations may be divided into 'traditional' issues and 'new' Issues.' Traditionally, GATT dealt with trade in manufactured goods and issues related to these, such as market access (tariffs and quotas), dumping, subsidies and disputes settlement. After the United Nations Conference on Trade and Development (UNCTAD) was formed in 1964, issues of concern to developing countries were added, such as commodities, transfer of technology, and terms of trade (I call them 'UNCTAD issues'). And then a number of issues were added with the signing of the Uruguay Agreement. At the same time, the UNCTAD issues were taken out.

The UNCTAD issues came on board largely at the behest of developing countries. Their origin was linked with the developing countries' dissatisfaction with the existing order and their call for a new dispensation-a New International Economic Order (NIEO). UNCTAD's creation was also closely associated with the ideas of Raùl Prebisch, its 'architect' and first Secretary-General. He, among others, developed a theory to counter mainstream growth theory. This counter-hegemonic theory is known by several names: 'underdevelopment' theory, the centre and periphery theory, or the Latin American Dependencia Theory.[16]

With the rise of neoliberal ideology in the 1980s and '90s, the idea of NIEO died, and the Dependencia School was marginalised.

Traditional Issues	UNCTAD Issues	WTO New Issues
Manufactured Goods	Commodities	Agricultural goods
Market access	Technology Transfer	Textile & Clothing
Dumping	Terms of Trade	Services
Subsidies	TNCs (Transnational	Intellectual Property
Industrial Tariffs	corporations)	Investment
Dispute Settlement		(TRIMS)
		Telecommunications
		Competition Policy
		Procurement
		Environment
		Labour Standards
		Trade Facilitation
		GMOs
		Development

And with these, the UNCTAD issues were taken out of the 'trade' agenda. UNCTAD is now a mere shadow of its original self, and the WTO, without the UNCTAD issues, has become a club of the rich and powerful.

A summary account of how these 'new issues' came onto the WTO agenda, and an explanation of what their present status is, might be useful to prepare the ground for further analysis in this and subsequent chapters.

New Issues on the WTO Agenda

Agriculture: For a long time, developed countries did not want to bring agriculture into the Multilateral Trading System. Each of them developed their own agriculture under protectionist barriers. The European Common Agricultural Policy (CAP), for example, was based on massive domestic and export subsidies. European farmers with political clout were resistant to allowing a liberalised market in agriculture because it would compromise their 'lifestyles.' By the 1980s, however, European domestic and export subsidies resulted in large crop surpluses and downward stress on food prices. Under pressure from the US, agriculture was put on the agenda of the Uruguay Round negotiations. The US and the EU worked out a compromise by which the developed countries would be allowed to retain trade-distorting subsidies that cause 'not more than minimal trade distortion'—whatever that means. The developing countries were on the side-line during agricultural negotiations. This is how agriculture came under WTO discipline.

Trade-Related Intellectual Property Rights (TRIPS): TRIPS came about largely as a result of pressure from the pharmaceutical industry in the US. They are not about free trade but about preserving monopolies. There are other conventions, such as the Convention on Biological

Diversity (CBD), that deal with intellectual property from the standpoint of protecting diversity, but these conventions are substantially negated by the TRIPS Agreement.

Services: These agreements refer to trade in non-visible commodities, including banking, insurance, shipping, catering, tourism, communications and a host of other issues. There is an effort to move some goods into the services sector by blurring essential distinctions—for example, food and catering, and carpets as goods versus carpeting as a service. A greater portion of the export revenue of developed countries now comes from services rather than from goods, and hence there is increasing pressure from them to expand the ambit of services in the WTO agenda.

Environment and Labour Standards: These have never been trade issues. There are other global institutions set up specifically to deal with them. But they were put on the agenda because Western corporations argued that developing countries' 'low wages' and 'low environmental standards' gave them an 'unfair' advantage, and therefore these should fall under WTO discipline in order to 'level the playing field.'

Investment Policy: This has never been a trade issue. Traditionally, it is in fact the IMF and the World Bank that deal with the movement of money and capital. Capital regulation and movement are certainly not a legitimate function of the WTO. However, investment policy squeezed itself onto the WTO agenda at the Singapore WTO conference as a result of pressure from American and European multinationals. This was finally removed from the WTO agenda at the 2003 Cancún Ministerial Conference.

Competition Policy: This too came under WTO discipline in Singapore, as one of the four so-called 'Singapore Issues.' This put at risk any type of policy options that developing countries could exercise in favour of their own natural enterprises. This was also removed from the WTO agenda at the Cancún Ministerial Conference.

Government Procurement: This is one of the four Singapore Issues. It should never have been within the WTO's ambit, but it was brought there, again, as a result of pressure from Western corporations. This put at risk developing countries' sovereignty to procure public goods from national sources. This too was removed from the WTO agenda at the Cancún Ministerial Conference.

Trade Facilitation: Also a Singapore Issue, trade facilitation is still on the WTO agenda. It is being exploited by the developed countries to pry open developing countries' economies under the excuse that they are 'simply' helping the developing countries to become more efficient in carrying out trade and getting integrated into the globalised market.

Three of the above-mentioned four Singapore Issues are now out of the WTO's ambit. However, developed countries are trying to smuggle in the 'lost' three issues through bilateral and regional trade agreements with developing countries, called Free Trade Areas (FTAs). For example, they are attempting to extend the 'principle of national treatment,' which applies to goods, to the investment sector. Developing countries have questioned the validity of such an extension.[17]

AGRICULTURE AND FOOD SECURITY
The Salience of Food Security in Agriculture

Since 1995 agriculture has been part of the WTO agenda, but food security is not. Market access, not food security, is the WTO's raison d'être. To an ordinary mind, this is a contradiction, but such is the surreal actuality of the trading system. It is too easy to forget that the WTO is a trade, not development, institution. Development was added to its agenda at the Doha Ministerial, and as stated earlier, the 'big and powerful' are trying their best to obliterate 'Development' from the 'Doha Development

Round' (DDR). It is assumed that development will follow trade. As Pascal Lamy said, 'Trade must be at the heart of Africa's recovery and growth in order to achieve the Millennium Development Goals (MDGs).' It is an ideological position that has very little to do with reality.

The DDR has twenty chapters, of which the most important are on agriculture, industry and services. All issues for negotiations have a political, a social, and an economic dimension. But whilst industry is primarily economic and services are primarily social, agriculture is primarily political. How so? Because a breakthrough in agriculture at the WTO is the basis on which negotiations in other areas may move, even if agriculture itself is contingent on agreement in these areas. This has been the case from the 1986 initiating conference at Punta del Este to the Bali Ministerial in 2013. History and economic logic show that no country can develop without industry and manufacturing. The WTO negotiations on NAMA (Non-Agricultural Market Access) are therefore crucial. If trade negotiators from developing countries get their industrial tariff coefficients wrong, they can bid goodbye to the industrialisation of their countries. In the case of services, if negotiators from the South underestimate the importance of their social dimension, then they will have a lot to answer for if their countries lose national control over health, education, transport, banking, and other services. But if agricultural negotiations go wrong, then governments, especially in the South, can potentially face angry electorates, or even lose power.

In 2008, the UN Special Rapporteur on the Right to Food, Jean Ziegler, reported that despite growth in some Southern countries, overall there has been little progress in reducing the number of victims of hunger and malnutrition. Hunger has increased every year since 1996 (reaching an estimated

rates' (tariff rates that are effective at a certain point in time) well below their 'bound rates' (upper limits allowed to them in order to protect their agriculture and industry), thus exposing their economies to imports and dumping.

THE COTTON WAR: THE CASE OF THE COTTON FOUR
Origins of the Case of the Cotton Four Countries

On 10 June 2003, at a meeting of the WTO's General Council, Burkina Faso, on behalf of the Cotton Four (Benin, Burkina Faso, Chad, and Mali), raised the issue of the serious damage caused to their economies by America's trade-distorting cotton subsidies.

Most analysts agree with the C-4 that the US's cotton subsidies are trade distorting: they result in at least a 10 percent reduction in global cotton prices. Earlier, the World Bank and Oxfam had argued that US subsidies also undermined the norms of special treatment to the LDCs.[22] Another study reported the following: 'Because of the prominent role cotton plays in the economies of C-4 . . . a small decline in cotton prices can make an enormous difference in the ability of their farmers to pay for health care, education, and food. A good price for cotton allows farmers to boost production of subsistence crops, slows urbanisation by keeping people in rural areas, and creates localised wealth in rural places that need it most.'[23] In the C-4, the cotton sector is the second-largest formal employer after the national states—approximately 900,000 farm units are engaged in providing employment to 7-to-8 million actively farming adults, and they support the livelihoods of the 10-to-13 million people (including children and non-farming adults) that comprise these farming units. Cotton also provides employment to workers in the associated agro-input, transportation and transformation industries.[24]

The C-4 countries' position is backed by the G20 developing countries and the whole of Africa. Uganda said a number of other African countries are in the same position as the C-4 and suggested that the number in the group's name could be increased to incorporate all the cotton-producing countries of Africa.

So What has the WTO done about it?

On 19 November 2004—soon after the C-4 had brought the matter before the WTO—its General Council had set up a body to focus on cotton. That was ten years ago. On 28 July 2009, the C-4 sent a high-level delegation to Washington to discuss the issue. They were listened to politely by a low-level official team, but they came back home empty-handed.

Also, because of America's persistent refusal to cooperate, the WTO body has made no progress. Before the 2013 WTO Bali Ministerial, the C-4 proposed to the General Council that the issue of distorting subsidies be settled by the end of 2014, that any remaining export subsidies on cotton in developed countries be eliminated immediately, and that the LDCs be given duty-free and quota-free access to the markets of developed countries.

To the now almost global demand that it remove trade-distorting subsidies on cotton, the US proposed an alternative strategy. In the 2013 IFDC's report 'Linking Cotton and Food Security in the Cotton-Four (C-4) Countries,' the USAID-funded body suggested that the 20 million food insecure people of the C-4 need aid (implying that this does not require the removal of US subsidy): 'The links between cotton and food security are complex ... Poverty and food insecurity are extremely high in these cotton economies. In that sense, producing and exporting cotton has not prevented food insecurity in the C-4 countries.'[25]

The IFDC study says, in other words, that in seeking an end to US cotton subsidies, the C-4 are barking up the wrong tree. The study points to a different tree: 'These findings suggest that improving food security in the C-4 countries requires sustained, coordinated interventions in the agricultural sectors (which provide both food and incomes for the large number of rural poor, and food for the urban populations). It also requires ongoing attention to the pressing issues of governance and civil insecurity, as well as a host of health and nutritional interventions.'

So the C-4 decided to try negotiating through the WTO. At the WTO Bali Ministerial (December 2013) they managed to get a statement in which the Ministers expressed 'regret' that 'we are yet to deliver' on the trade-related components of the Hong Kong Declaration; that the Declaration nonetheless provides 'a useful basis for our future work'; that the WTO would organise 'dedicated sessions' to enhance 'transparency and monitoring' of trade-related aspects of cotton; and that the DG of the WTO would 'provide periodic reports on the development assistance aspects of cotton.' *There was no mention that the US subsidies were trade-distorting and therefore, in WTO legal parlance, illegal.*

What should the C-4 do now? Should they take the matter to the WTO Disputes Settlement body (DSB)? In theory, every member state of the WTO has recourse to the DSB if it feels that its rights have been adversely affected by the action, or lack of action, of another country. But that is at the level of formal equality of membership. On the ground, the reality is very different. In real life, power and wealth count. Assume that the DSB decides in favour of the C-4. Then what? Then . . . well, nothing. Under the WTO there is no provision for collective sanctions. The DSB can make a judicial determination but it has no sanctions power—this is left to the aggrieved party or parties. The US might even accept the panel's decision, and then challenge the C-4 to impose sanctions against the US. What sanctions can the C-4 impose on the US? The C-4 can hoist a moral flag but it will not make any material difference to the case in dispute. This does not mean that small and weak states should not have recourse to the DSB. They should. But they should also be realistic.

What conclusion does one draw from this? There can be only one. There is no chance that the C-4 will win this war with the WTO. The Bali Declaration is only meant to placate the C-4 countries. They are up against a Goliath. It is a one-sided war.

The C-4 Should Develop Their Own Textile Industry

So here is an alternative suggestion: the C-4 should follow the example of India and China. These two countries are among the world's largest cotton producers. But instead of exporting cotton, they use it domestically for their own textile and associated industries. The C-4, in association with West and Central African countries, might put their heads and resources together and work out a five- to ten-year strategy for how to reduce cotton exports and shift to domestic and regional value addition, i.e., to developing their own textile industries. Of course, this is not simple. Nothing is. But it can be done. Since I come from Uganda, I would also suggest that Uganda and the other cotton-producing countries in Africa recommend that the African Union and the UN Economic Commission for Africa set up a group of agro-industrial experts to help with this process—that of moving from exporting raw cotton to using it within Africa for its own manufacturing industrialisation.

THE DEVELOPMENT ISSUE

This is one of the most contentious issues of our time. The very definition of development is a battleground, let alone the related issues of policy and its implementation at various levels—local, national, regional, and global. There is much talk in some circles about creating a 'development state,' where both words are contested.

The MDGs Reduce Development to Numbers

However, here we need not enter this complex conceptual and operational terrain, except to note that within the context of the UN system the concept of 'development' has been reduced to a numbers game without any depth.[26] The Millennium Development Goals (MDGs) are a typical UN exercise in reaching a 'compromise,' thus avoiding contested concepts in favour of reaching some shared goals and milestones. Of course, there is nothing wrong in setting such goals and development indicators. The MDGs have certainly put the issue of poverty on the global media map, but by the same token they have also served to distract attention from the systemic and structural causes of poverty and underdevelopment. I agree with Manuel Montes: 'The big attraction of the eight Millennium Development Goals (MDGs), or at least the first seven of these, was their near-universal acceptability. It mobilised both resources and politics, both nationally and internationally, in pursuit of reducing poverty, hunger, gender inequality, malnutrition, and disease. Since they were introduced, the excitement over the MDGs fully occupied the space for development thinking. The MDG discourse—in international agencies and in national settings—appears to have crowded out the basic idea that development is about economic transformation . . . . De-Colonising the MDGs is necessary if the agreed goals are to be truly developmental.'[27]

The MDG period ends with 2015. Statistical data from the United Nations and OECD sources about how far these have been achieved are like smoke and mirrors. At the Rio+20 Conference in 2012, the UN launched the so-called 'Sustainable Development Goals (SDGs)' as its post-2015 development agenda. Once again, this did not address underlying structural causes of continuing underdevelopment of the countries of the South. It is early to assess this but any thinking person analysing the SDGs would see that the UN is simply changing the goal posts from MDGs to SDGs.

UNCTAD's Lost Development Agenda Resurrected

It is assumed by the WTO that development will follow trade. But then the question is, by what processes do matters get on the 'trade' agenda, and who gets what in the course of the trade negotiations?

We saw that in the 1960s the UNCTAD brought up issues related to commodities, technology transfer, terms of trade and transnational corporations, but over a period, especially with the onset of the Washington Consensus in the mid-1980s, these were quietly put aside. At the WTO Doha Ministerial in 2001, 'Development' was put on the WTO agenda. So the present situation is that, as they did with 'UNCTAD issues,' the developed countries of the West are trying their best to obliterate development from the 'Doha (Development) Round' (DDR), especially the matter of Special and Differential Treatment (S&D) for the less-developed economies.

The Long Losing Fight over S&D

Let us recall that S&D is a recognised principle that goes back to the WTO's pre-history—to the 1986 Punta del Este Declaration. Its Part IX: Article 15 states that: 'In keeping with the recognition that differential and more favourable treatment for developing country Members is an integral part of the negotiation, special and differential treatment in respect of commitments shall be provided as set out in the relevant provisions of this Agreement and embodied in the Schedules of concessions and commitments.' And, further: 'Developing country Members shall have the flexibility to implement reduction commitments over a period of up to 10 years. Least-developed country Members shall not be required to undertake reduction commitments.'

But the S&D principle was given very little legal weight at the conclusion of the Uruguay Round. Most issues of interest to developed countries have an *obligatory* character, with the weight of the DSB and the sanctions system behind them. This, however, is not the case with the S&D provisions. These are under the '*best endeavour*' commitments of the WTO system—members will try their best, but they have no binding obligation to do so. This weakness of S&D has been recognised for a long time. At Doha, finally, Members agreed that 'all Special and Differential Treatment provisions shall be reviewed with a view to strengthening them and making them more precise, effective and operational.' Following Doha, the WTO set up a Committee on Trade and Development (CTD). Later, in 2002, the CTD set up a Monitoring Mechanism (MM) to follow through discussion and implementation of the development aspect of the Doha Round, especially the issue of 'strengthening' the S&D provisions.

That was the last that anybody heard of 'strengthening' the provisions of the S&D. The WTO's Ninth Ministerial Conference at Bali carried out a systematic destruction of the S&D provisions, except in name. The reasons for this annihilation of S&D are fully comprehensible under the present circumstances of intense pressure on the developed countries of the North to gain access to the markets and resources of the South. At Bali, developed countries were focused on 'trade facilitation' (the one remaining issue of the four Singapore Issues) and were not in the mood to give concessions to developing countries or the LDCs on the basis of 'strengthening' the S&D provisions.

The language of the Bali Declaration is quite unambiguous in this regard. In defining the 'Functions/Terms of Reference' of the MM, the Bali Declaration states: 'The Mechanism shall review all aspects of implementation of S&D provisions with a view to facilitating integration of developing and least-developed Members into the multilateral trading system.' The objective is to facilitate the South's 'integration' into the MTS, not protect it from special and differential considerations. The declaration made it clear: 'The Mechanism will complement, not replace, other relevant review mechanisms and/or processes in other bodies of the WTO.' In case the MM did not understand this, it added in a footnote: 'Members will have the discretion to avail themselves of the Mechanism as well as other relevant review mechanisms or processes in other bodies of the WTO.' The declaration went on: 'In carrying out its functions, the Mechanism will not alter, or in any manner affect, Members' rights and obligations under WTO Agreements, Ministerial or General Council Decisions, or interpret their legal nature.' . . . *meaning the MM must keep out of substantive matters of trade discourse reserved for the big and powerful.* But in a gesture of conciliation, the declaration relented a bit: 'However, the Mechanism is not precluded from making recommendations to the relevant WTO bodies for initiating negotiations on the S&D provisions that have been reviewed under the Mechanism.' But it quickly set the tone in case the MM had any illusions on this matter: '*Such recommendations will inform the work of the relevant body, but not define or limit its final determination.*' It is necessary to read the language of the Bali text very carefully to understand that 'development' is all but obliterated from the WTO.

CONCLUSION

The WTO, like all multilateral agencies, is driven by certain balance of economic, Ideological, and political forces in the global domain. Asymmetrical power relations are part of the dynamics of global negotiations and outcomes. The South suffered a significant loss as a result of the weakening of the UNCTAD, the emergence of neoliberal globalisation and the collapse of the Soviet Union.

The weight of evidence and my own experience show that the WTO is an extended arm of US and EU trade and foreign policy. Japan used to be in this league, but has become a second-rate power. Brazil, Russia, India and China (BRIC) are, as newly industrialising countries, significant players, but they still have limited clout in the WTO. The most significant explanation is that the WTO was crafted by the US and EU, and there are structurally embedded aspects of the WTO that are resistant to change, except where it suits Western interests.

In the WTO, Europe is the most aggressive player. It has a vigorous and aggressive secretariat in Brussels, driven by the Global Europe strategy, which is closely monitored and directed by BusinessEurope.[28] Despite outward opulence, Europe is in a serious economic and financial crisis, and is more vulnerable than the US to the risk of losing markets and access to oil and raw materials. Europe must secure access to these, not only in the old empire but also in the growing economies of Brazil, China, India, Russia and South Africa.

The South is, of course, not as united as Europe. Europe speaks with one voice in the WTO, the South with more than a hundred. What unites the countries of the South is their shared experience of colonialism and the sense of injustice in the trading system; what divides them is their disparate national interests. Sometimes the South manages to sing in harmony, but when the 'big ones' among them are cajoled into the 'green room' processes of the WTO, the harmony breaks down, and Europe and the US are quick to take advantage of this. At the 2001 (Doha), 2005 (Hong Kong), and 2013 (Bali) Ministerials, for example, the big developing countries were so preoccupied with protecting their own interests that despite all the solidarity among their negotiators in Geneva, this unity broke down under political pressure. However, unlike during the Uruguay Round negotiations, the developing countries are now more engaged, and are able to resist pressures and unfair demands on them, like in Seattle (1999), Cancun (2003), and Geneva (2009 and 2011).

African countries are among the weakest. This weakness is not in their negotiating skills. In Geneva, African negotiators have shown remarkable unity and bargaining skills over the years. African weakness lies in the capitals and in their political leadership. The officials and politicians are easy targets of both political pressure (especially from Europe) and aid dependency. Corruption is part of it, but the bigger danger Africa faces is so-called 'development aid,' for it robs Africa of an independent economic policy. Aid brings in its wake 'policy distortions' such as the Structural Adjustment Programs (SAPs). *Bribes corrupt bureaucrats and politicians; but aid corrupts state polices.* On the other hand, the civil society organisations (NGOs) working on trade, debt and development issues are not insignificant players. They are able, at times, to push their bureaucracy and political leaders to protect and advance Africa's interests in global trade negotiations (we shall see more of this in the next chapter).

The WTO is a trade negotiating forum. Its assumption that development is a by-product of trade is based on an untenable neoliberal ideology. There is no empirical evidence to support this assumption. In fact, unfettered trade polarises nations between the rich and the poor. Ironically, while the rich advocate free markets for poor countries, they practice protection, as we saw earlier in the case of agriculture. There is a discourse about 'fair trade,' especially among NGOs, but within the WTO context, it is a red herring.

The WTO is not as benign and neutral as it is often made out to be. Its rules are subject to change at the behest of the powerful. At the Uruguay Round, the US and the EU agreed to bring in agriculture as part of the GATT, having provided each other certain leeway to impose trade-distorting subsidies. But now, US and EU agricultural subsidies are a major factor in increasing hunger in the Global South. Above all, the US and EU are able to manipulate trade rules and 'shift' between amber, blue, and green boxes and *de minimis* to increase, not decrease, their subsidies. The US refuses to remove trade-distorting subsidy to its cotton producers, irrespective of its threat to the lives of millions in Africa. In this light, its African Growth and Opportunities Act (AGOA) is insincere and hypocritical.

The WTO is a veritable battleground where the warring parties fight over real issues—as lethal in their impact on the lives of millions in the South as 'real wars.' Trade kills. The big and powerful employ sophisticated weapons—technical arguments, legalisms, and ideological and political weapons with deftness and chicanery—as lethal as drone attacks. The US and EU change the rules of the WTO as they go along. For example, the principle of 'single undertaking' is a means to ensure that there is a 'balanced outcome' at the end of negotiations. But increasingly, the US and

EU have attempted to change the architecture of the Doha Round's single undertaking in order to 'early harvest' some issues to their advantage. And when the Multilateral Trading System (MTS) does not suit their interests, they turn to 'plurilaterals' in the WTO and to bilateral or regional Free Trade Agreements (FTAs) outside the WTO. One of these, the European attempt to get an Economic Partnership Agreement (EPA), is the subject of the next chapter.

3. EPAs: EUROPE'S TRADE WAR ON AFRICA

To understand Africa, it is necessary to understand Europe, just like to understand the poor you have to understand the rich.

INTRODUCTION:
THREE ENDURING FEATURES OF EURO-AFRICAN RELATIONS

In 1884 Europe carved up Africa on a map and proceeded to conquer it. The old civilisations of Africa were destroyed and new commoditised relations at all levels were introduced by the invading powers. Since the so-called 'independence' of African nations in the 1960s, the commoditisation of African economies has been accelerating. Capitalist relations have now been internalised by the entire population of the continent. Post-independence, Europe simply altered the form of its relations with Africa, but not the content.

The Euro-African relationship has three basic enduring features:

1. It is a relationship based on power asymmetry. Those that abstract economics from power (as economists tend to do) have only a partial understanding of what drives that relationship; economics is significant but it is not the whole story.
2. It is a relationship built over a century and deeply embedded in the institutions, culture, and behaviour of both sides of

the divide. It will take a long time of consciously willed and organised struggle to break away from what essentially is a dependent culture on one side and a domineering, imperial culture on the other. Some progress has been made in this direction over the last fifty years (since Ghana became independent in 1957), but there is still a long way to go.

3. The colonially constructed discourse and terms of negotiation persist to this day. The importance of this point cannot be overemphasised. The essential terms to understand in their proper historical context are: 'preference,' 'reciprocity,' and 'non-reciprocity.' These later became a part of the WTO's vocabulary.

Where did all this begin? To comprehend the present, you have to know the past.

PART ONE: THE HISTORICAL CONTEXT
The Imperial System of 'Preference' as a Form of Trade War
Imperial 'preferences': a conceptual trap

The current relationship between Africa and Europe began in June 2000 when the Cotonou Agreement was signed between Africa and Europe. REPAs (later changed to EPAs, a subtle distinction whose significance I shall explain later) were to be negotiated after 2008—to replace non-reciprocal preferences with a reciprocal relationship. Why? Because it was argued that the European 'preferences' for Africa were incompatible with the WTO principle of reciprocity, and unfair to the rest of the trading community, especially other countries of the South—such as the Philippines and Costa Rica—that did not 'enjoy' such preferences.

It is therefore important to understand the meaning of 'preference' and 'non-reciprocity.' When and why did these terms become part of the vocabulary of international trade? How did non-reciprocity become an aspect of the preferential trade regime? *Was the 'preference' given to Africa really preferential?* Was it a 'concession' given by Europe to Africa? Or was it, perhaps, the other way around, a preference given by (or taken from) African nations to the imperial countries that controlled their economies? The questions are rhetorical, of course. But just to raise them is significant.

Non-reciprocity has roots in the imperial system of preferences

What passes under the name of 'preference' today has its roots in the colonial system where Africa served imperial interests at the cost of the colonies. What were the needs of imperial Europe during the colonial period?

There were essentially three:

1. Cheap commodities for European industries in competition with other imperial countries;
2. A market for manufactured products;
3. Control over money and credit as the basis of capital accumulation.

And how were these needs satisfied by (or extracted from) the colonies? This was done by four means:

1. By force of arms to transform pre-colonial societies to serve imperial interests;
2. By establishing an imperial system of governance at the political level;
3. By establishing a structure of financial, banking, transport and insurance services to enable the financing and transport of goods to and from the colonies; and

4.   By establishing a 'preferential' system at the economic level, so that colonial products had 'preferential' access to, for example, England as opposed to Japan.

In its very origin, then, the idea of 'preference' is in fact a conceptual trap. It is presented today as a 'concession' to Africa; in reality it has always been, and remains, a concession by Africa to Europe. During colonial days Uganda, for example, was forbidden from exporting its coffee or cotton to, say, Japan or Germany, even if under the 'free market' they offered higher prices. Preferences, rather than free trade, suited imperial interests—not those of the colonies.

The role of 'preferences' in sustaining Europe during the interwar period

How did African 'preferences' (as opposed to free trade) for imperial Europe sustain the latter during the interwar years (1918–39) and during the 1939–45 war? Europe was at 'peace' during the interwar period. But under the surface there was another war simmering between the British and the Americans. In the nineteenth century, the British exploited the American colonies to secure commodities—such as cotton and tobacco—for their industries. After America won its independence in 1776, the US wanted these for its own industrialisation. England lost both a source of commodities and a market. This was one reason behind its colonisation of Africa. It needed to secure an alternative source of industrial commodities—for example, cotton from Uganda. And it needed to develop a market for British industrial products.

In the 1930s, Europe and America went into deep economic depression. At the domestic level, John Maynard Keynes's theories (in England) and Roosevelt's New Deal theories (in the US) addressed similar challenges arising out of the depression of the

1930s. At the international level, however, they were at war—war over currency and markets. Keynes's biographer Robert Skidelsky explains how, *in order to protect imperial trade preferences*, England mobilised twenty-five of its colonies to join a downward float against the dollar. Skidelsky's justification for this protective action against the dollar is fascinating. He says, 'It was all the fault of the Americans.' By maintaining a high tariff, America had made it extremely difficult for England to export to it and repay its debts to America.[29]

The rivalry for markets and resources between Britain and the United States exploded into a 'full-blown economic war.' The US refused to accept the sterling's depreciation as a defensive act by England. The US suspected Britain was using its Exchange Equalisation Fund to keep it undervalued and undercut American exports. In retaliation, the US suspended dollar convertibility into gold in April 1933, despite ample reserves.[30]

One thing comes out clearly from Skidelsky's story about the US-UK wrangle during the interwar period; namely, that the currency manipulation and the preferential system were to protect imperial Britain, and not the colonies, against the predatory and protectionist United States.

How Africa saved Europe during the Second World War

What most Western historians miss—and this is very important—is that it was the colonies (not the US) that sustained Europe not only during the interwar years but also, significantly, during the inter-imperialist Second World War. Africa did this through:

- Supplying vital foods and commodities to sustain the war effort and the soldiers fighting at the front;
- Currency and monetary support;

- At the war front in Africa and Asia, thousands of soldiers from the colonies perished, not to mention the huge physical carnage in African countries where the Europeans fought their proxy wars.[31]

It is a fascinating story which colonial historians either gloss over or treat casually. Let me explore the example of Uganda during the Second World War. Between 1941 and 1945, the British instituted 'bulk purchasing schemes' for the production, marketing, and export of cotton and coffee. The entire crop of coffee was bought under a monopoly scheme by the Uganda Coffee Marketing Board. British exporters paid Uganda peasants £150 per ton and then sold it in the global market for £800–1000 per ton.[32] This is gross profiteering by any measure. In the case of cotton, ginning companies became agents of the British state—prices were fixed, crops were bulk purchased, and the colonial government organised an 'Exporters Group' to export cotton at prices set by the British state in collaboration with the British cotton monopoly interests. At the time it might have suited the people of Uganda to trade with the 'enemies'—Germany and Japan—and secure better prices, but this was forbidden not only because Uganda too (through no choice of its own) was 'at war' with Germany and Japan, but also because of the pre-war imperial 'preferences' system that was embedded in the colonial economic infrastructure.

America and Europe continue their war over Africa's markets and resources
During the Second World War, as part of the collective war effort, the US provided—under a financing scheme called 'Lend-Lease Aid'—$50.1 billion (equivalent to about $650 billion today) worth of military supplies to Britain, France, the USSR, China, and other

allied countries.[33] But the US 'aid' had a price tag. Getting on its moral high horse (recalling Woodrow Wilson's First World War call for 'national self-determination' for the colonies), the US demanded that in return for its 'aid' Britain and France must free their colonies in Asia and Africa. For the colonies, it was music to the ears—an ideology for their liberation. But for the US it was, in essence, an imperial ideology—a music of a different sort—a strategy of forcing the imperial countries (especially Britain and France) to open up their territories to US goods and investments as part of its so-called 'open door policy.' Stripped of its moral cloak, the Lend-Lease Aid to Europe was a smart way of telling its wartime allies that if you do away with imperial preferences, we'll give you a few billion dollars of military supplies.[34]

The Lend-Lease aid was followed, immediately after the war, by the Marshall Plan to help Europe recover from the war.[35] It is now generally known that its real aim was geopolitical—namely, to prevent the spread of Communism by building up Europe's industrial base. The Marshall Plan is almost always projected in present day economics literature as a 'model' for aid donors to follow in relation to Africa.[36] On closer scrutiny, it turns out not to be as good a model as it is made out to be. It is well recognised that it was a self-enlightened plan aimed mainly at enabling Western countries (including Germany) and Japan to recover economically in order to face up to the challenge of the Soviet Union and what then looked like its unstoppable march towards occupying Eastern and Central Europe, right to the gates of Berlin.

Immediately, after the war, the US quickly set out to create a global economic infrastructure to establish its hegemony, namely GATT (a reduced version of the failed attempt to create the ITO), the IBRD (World Bank), the IMF, and most significantly, the US dollar as an international reserve currency 'as good as gold.'

Skidelsky has an interesting account of the struggle between the declining British power and the emerging US power to shape the emerging world, a battle which the British were destined by history to lose.[37]

Europe adopted a two-track strategy to avert the threat of multilateralism and the open-door policy pursued by the US. The first was to work with the US in the areas of security and military cooperation. European countries joined NATO in 1949 (although, in reality, Europe left much of the burden of fighting the threat from the Soviet Union to the US. This was later to become a contentious issue—that of 'burden sharing'—between the US and Europe). The second track of this strategy was to protect imperial preferences from the threat of encroachment by the US. To this end, Europe created 'special relations' with the former colonies in the form of the British Commonwealth and *Francophonie*. Each had its own peculiarities. The British Commonwealth had the Queen as its head, and in some countries, like in most countries in the Caribbean, the Queen was even the head of state, represented by a 'governor.' In the case of *Francophonie*, the French encouraged a local elite class in the neo-colonies to become members of the ruling class in France. More importantly, Europe tied the former colonies' currencies to imperial currencies—the pound sterling and the franc. Through this, Britain and France were not only able to control the money supply in the former colonies, but also, through an elaborate banking and credit (and 'aid') system, they controlled the production and marketing of the resources Europe needed to continue to service the needs of European corporations.

As the United States got more and more engaged in the military and security aspects of the Atlantic alliance, Europe consolidated its economic and financial domination of a large part of its former empire, mostly in Africa, the Caribbean and the Pacific

Islands. Other former colonies—those in Asia—managed to fight for their relative economic independence. India and Malaysia, for example, joined the Commonwealth but they were not tied to British trade preferences or its currency systems. In the case of Vietnam, its people had to fight a war of liberation, first against the French and then against the United States. Much of this historical information is ignored in contemporary analysis when comparing Asian growth figures with the relative backwardness of Africa.[38]

PART TWO: CONTEMPORARY EURO-AFRICAN TRADE RELATIONS
Structural Effects on Africa of the 'Preference' System

The imperial 'preference' system was, in reality, a case of 'reverse preference'—a system that favoured Europe, not Africa. And yet, by a strange ironical (or cynical) twist, Africans were (and still are) made to believe that they owed (still owe) their survival to the 'preferences' that they 'enjoyed' ('enjoy') in the European market. In a bizarre sense, this is true; it is like the slave who is in debt to the 'preferences' the slave owner gives him so that the slave survives in order to serve his master.

The structural effects of this odious 'preference' system are obvious. The colonial economy has become an annex to the imperial economy—and this persists to this day, fifty years after Africa's political (but not economic) liberation. The Empire extracts resources (agricultural and mineral) and exploits cheap labour from the colonies for its industrialisation whilst the latter are structurally 'underdeveloped.' The neo-colonies produce what they cannot use or consume (like cotton and cocoa) and they import from the Empire finished goods (like processed foods, textiles and engineering products). In the long run, 'preferences' created structures of colonial dependence on the Empire—from the production of goods and services, to financial structures (banking and finance), taxation and fiscal policies, the education structure, systems of governance, language, culture, and above all, the thinking of the elite placed in power to service the needs of the Empire. It is a colossal structure of dependence masquerading as 'preference.'

This point is worth keeping in mind, for it has a bearing when we come to examining the current state of negotiations on Economic Partnership Agreements (EPAs). Take the case of bananas, for example. Because of the 'preference' system, Britain imported these from Africa and the Caribbean, France from Cote d'Ivoire and Cameroon and the 'Overseas Departments' of Guadeloupe and Martinique, and Italy from Somalia. When the 'preference' system had to be dismantled under the WTO regime, the former colonies faced the prospect of losing their duty-free access to Europe. Caribbean small-scale farmers complained that the loss of 'preference' would subject them to competition from the large plantation producers like Del Monte in the Philippines and Central America, with devastating effects for several Caribbean economies. Bananas became a major issue of contention between the African, Caribbean, and Pacific (ACP) countries and the European Union in the 1990s.[39]

Or take sugar. During the 'Cold War' period, a country like Mauritius, for example, could export 100 percent of its sugar to Europe at higher than world prices. So the entire economy was sugar-dependent and in turn Europe-dependent. When time came to align Mauritius export prices to world prices, it had to undertake a structural transformation of its entire economy.

Bananas, sugar, cotton, and beef are some of the major items of colonial production that face huge challenges because of the dependence on them created by the imperial system of 'preferences.' The entire restructuring of the 'preference' system is a nightmare—it is like reversing the course of the last hundred years of history.

The Background to the Cotonou Agreement

One of the most contentious issues in relations between Africa and Europe is agriculture—the production and trade in food and agricultural commodities. Africa needs food for its survival, and other commodities for its industrialisation. The United States was able, after 1776, to take control of commodities such as cotton and sugar for its industrialisation. In the contemporary geopolitical and economic situation, Europe cannot allow Africa to go the American route, as the following account will show.

One of the difficulties facing Europe is the new trading system inaugurated by the Uruguay Round Agreements (URA). Europe had succeeded all these years in keeping agriculture out of the trading system. It was not included in the old GATT. Under pressure from the US, agriculture was brought under the URA in 1995, and thus within the ambit of the WTO. The US contended that under the WTO, the Common Agricultural Policy (CAP) was 'market distorting.' Europe was obliged to end the 'preferential' trade regime for the ACP countries.

Under the old CAP, the EU had provided imperial 'preferences' to the former colonies so that they produced essential foods (beef, bananas, sugar, etc.) for Europe at guaranteed prices that were higher than world market prices. This was to ensure food security for Europe in the context of the Cold War. Within Europe itself, the policy was to sustain high-cost and market-inefficient (market-distorting) producers through minimum grower prices guaranteed by subsidies, and through dumping incidental surpluses on the world market with export rebates. Thus, food security for Europe in the dangerous times of the Cold War was a *strategic* objective. The cost in financial terms was heavy, but it was considered justified under circumstances then prevailing. The cost in terms of creating dependence in ACP countries was also high, but at the time it was presented to the ACP countries as a special 'concession' to them.

When the Cold War was over by 1991, the high cost of storage and export refund payments was no longer justified at the domestic (that is, EU) level. Nor was the 'preferential treatment' to the ACP countries defensible. Faced with this situation, Europe prioritised protecting its own farmers. In 1992 a fundamental shift was made in CAP from the system of price support to one of direct aid to farmers. The aim was to reduce domestic prices of agricultural products, without eroding farm incomes. This was seen as WTO-compatible, since it was deemed *less* trade distorting under green- or blue-box measures.[40] Furthermore, price reduction and the closing of the gap between EU and world market prices provided an incentive to EU processors of agricultural products to produce for export. Indeed, this is one of the main objectives of the new CAP. Under pressure from food-processing industries, the objective is to provide primary agricultural inputs into the European food industry, targeted at capturing a share of the world market in processed foods.

Europe needs Africa's market and resources—more than the US for example. With the entry of China in Africa, Europe has much to lose because of its relatively uncompetitive trading position vis-à-vis China. It is through using its so-called 'development aid,' investment, and technology that Europe can compete against China as well as against India and Brazil. Above all, it is the historically structured relationship with Africa that Europe tries to use to maximise its privileged position against its global competitors.

It is against this backdrop that Europe set out to weave its spider's web for Africa.

EU-ACP Cotonou Trade Agreement: An Unequal Treaty
Yaoundé begat Lomé and Lomé begat Cotonou

The first trade agreement between the European Commission (EC) and Europe's francophone former colonies in Africa was signed in Yaoundé, Cameroon in 1963. In 1969 the EC signed a separate agreement with the three Great Lakes-region countries of East Africa (Kenya, Uganda and Tanzania) called the Arusha Agreement. The EC also signed similar agreements with other former colonies in the Caribbean and the Pacific. During the 1970s, the EC decided to bring all these African, Caribbean and Pacific (ACP) countries into a common trading system.

In 1974, ACP and EC negotiators met in Dar es Salaam (at what was then called the Kilimanjaro Hotel) to negotiate what later came to be called Lomé I. Shridath Ramphal, then Guyana's Foreign Minister, was the lead negotiator for the ACP countries. At the time, Professor Dani Nabudere and I were teachers at the University of Dar es Salaam.[41] Later, we heard from the corridors of Kilimanjaro that Ramphal was a good negotiator, and had put up a good fight, but the EU had flexed its political and aid muscle and Lomé I came out as a poor deal for Africa. Nabudere later wrote a book on Lomé called *Lomé Convention and the Crisis of Neocolonialisms: An Evaluation of Lomé I–III*.[42] It is still one of the best contemporary critiques of Lomé; its basic argument is still valid to this day.

Lomé was superseded, in 2000, by the Cotonou Agreement between seventy-nine ACP countries and the European Union. In other words, Yaoundé begat Lomé and Lomé begat Cotonou.[43] All these countries were in the tight neocolonial grip of the EU. The

Cotonou Agreement (CA) is, to this day, the principal framework agreement between Europe and Africa. Signed in 2000, the CA was designed to last for a period of twenty years.

Essentially, it is based on six main principles:

1. The principle of equality: the EU and the ACP countries recognise one another's sovereignty in negotiating trade agreements;
2. The principle of differentiation: the negotiations will take into account the level of development of each country, in particular that of the LDCs and landlocked or island states;
3. The principle of regionalisation: the CA recognises the ACP countries' long-term development strategy of regionalisation;
4. The principle of mutual obligations: each side must make commitments as agreed during the course of the negotiations;
5. The principle of participation: participation by non-state actors such as civil society groups, the private sector and local governments; and
6. The principle of respect for human rights, monitored through continuing dialogue and evaluation.

An unequal treaty

I will go into the implementation of the CA later in the chapter.[44] I will show that despite the above recognised principles of equality and mutual respect, the CA is an 'unequal treaty.' It is basically an agreement between two asymmetrical 'power blocs,' the (real) power of the fifteen (now twenty-seven) countries of the European Union, speaking with one voice coordinated from Brussels, pitted against the (fictitious) power of the seventy ACP countries, speaking with many voices. Europe has a single market; a standardised system of laws that apply in all member states; the free movement of people, goods, services and capital; common policies on trade, agriculture, fisheries and regional development; a monetary union, the Eurozone; and a common foreign and security policy.[45] The ACP countries have very diverse geographic, demographic and economic characteristics. Their per capita GDP ranges from about $9000 in some Caribbean countries to less than $100 in the poorest African countries.

Europe has a vigorous and aggressive secretariat in Brussels, driven by 'the Global Europe strategy,' which is closely monitored and directed by BusinessEurope.[46] One could argue that this monitoring and directing from outside of the EC is akin to a *corporate war council*. By contrast, the ACP has no real secretariat. The only 'coordination' for the ACP takes place in the 'ACP House' in Brussels along with ACP ambassadors based in European capitals. They try their best under the circumstances, but they are often at the mercy of the largesse the EC provides for the maintenance of the ACP House, and the per diems that the EC provides from time to time in order for them to meet and to attend workshops and international conferences. Most of the ACP countries are so financially strained that many of them depend on the EU and 'donor aid' from other countries to balance their national budgets. So they are quite happy for their officials at the ACP House in Brussels to be financed by the very body, the EC, with which they enter into negotiations about the future of their national and regional economies.

The substance of the Cotonou agreement

Coming to the substance of the Cotonou Agreement (CA), the first thing to understand is that it is not about the ACP countries' welfare or development. It is about the EU trying to maintain its competitiveness in the world market against the US, Japan, and—increasingly China and other newly industrialised countries. This is the essence of the CA and of Euro-ACP relations. The result, foreseen from the analysis of the EPAs, is clear. Europe benefits most and also locks in its competitive edge, which would be under threat if Africa integrated itself first. Evidence of the UN Economic Commission for Africa (ECA) fully supports this argument.[47]

In light of this, it is interesting to see how Europe has dealt with Africa's welfare and development needs. Although market access to Europe is important, Africa's main preoccupation is the protection of its economy against assault from outside. Africa' issues, in terms of priority, are:

1. Food sovereignty based on domestic production, and control over the basic means of production, such as land, water, seeds, and technology.

2. Agriculture as, first and foremost, a livelihood issue. 70–75 percent of Africa's population depends on it. A foolish and hasty step towards liberalisation can put at risk the livelihood of these people, most of them very poor. The LDCs, for example, are given preferential tariff-free and quota-free (TFQF) access to the European market, but in return they are required to liberalise their trade regime in food and agriculture. Whilst very few of the LDCs are able to take advantage of the TFQF (because of so-called supply constraints), they are hostages to food and agricultural imports (including dumping) from European and other countries.

3. However, smallholder farming as it is now cannot transform Africa. It is incumbent on Africa to transform agriculture so that it becomes 'industrialised.' Africa has to develop its own capacity to produce fertilisers, tractors, combine harvesters, irrigation equipment, and other industrial inputs into agriculture so that industry and agriculture move in tandem. The

colonially structured division of labour has located agriculture in Africa and industry in Europe.

4. The removal of imbalances and asymmetries in the WTO in relation to agriculture. For example, the African countries are not able to provide domestic support to their agriculture, not only because of budgetary constraints, but also, for many of them, because of the IMF and donor conditionalities. Also, Africa has no access to the so-called 'green-box' protection against imports from outside, even as the EC, hypocritically, talks about free trade.

5. Commodity prices and terms of trade[48] have moved against Africa in a long-term secular trend over the last thirty years, and the prices of commodities (including food) have gyrated wildly in recent years, causing a loss of revenue, escalating food and fuel prices, and food riots.

6. Indigenous knowledge and the threat of genetically modified organisms (GMOs) to local seed varieties is a matter of great concern to Africa, one that has almost slipped from the agenda of trade negotiations. Africa also has other concerns, such as: opposition to the patenting of life forms; sovereignty in making regulations affecting food security and health; concerns about the protection of biodiversity enshrined in the Convention on Bio-Diversity (CBD); and the protection of farmers' rights.

7. Appropriate levels of protection from agriculture dumping by Europe, and a reduction of subsidies to European farmers. The EC has often talked about decreasing subsidies to agriculture; actually, it has increased these over the years, and they are still increasing. Furthermore, the CAP reform makes EU products price-competitive because it replaces export subsidies with direct aid to farmers.

8.   Market access for agro-processed industrial products, especially for non-LDC countries such as South Africa, Kenya and Mauritius.

And so to the question is: how responsive is Europe to Africa's priorities? The answer is that the Cotonou Agreement has effectively reversed the order of priority by placing the last item (8 in the above list) first and the first item at the bottom of the pile. To be more precise, the CA deals only with the eighth issue on the list—all the remaining seven are pushed out of the agenda. Agriculture is treated as simply a tradable commodity, and the issue of market access becomes the core of all negotiations.

REPA, EPA, IEPA, FEPA, CEPA: the distorting mirrors of the EC's acronyms
The original concept used in the Cotonou Agreement (CA) was that of Regional Economic Partnership Agreements (REPAs). Slowly, the 'R' in REPAs was dropped. How did this happen, and why is it important to know this? The principle of regional integration is very important for the ACP countries. Article 35.2 of the CA states: "Economic and trade cooperation shall build on regional integration initiatives of ACP States, bearing in mind that regional integration is a key instrument for the integration of the ACP countries into the world economy (Article 35.2)." The Cotonou timetable of phased negotiations was as follows:

1.   Start-up process: ACP-wide consultations, regional consultations;
2.   ACP Action Plan;
3.   ACP Procedural Guidelines for Preparation and Negotiation of New Trade Arrangements;
4.   Capacity Building in Support of Preparation of Economic Partnership Agreements;

5.   Phase I—Action Plan from January 2001 to September 2002;

6.   Phase II—2004–06: Substantive Negotiations;

7.   Phase III—2007: Concluding and Signing.

The first item on the agenda was regional consultations, and the fourth item was capacity building. The first was carried out most superficially and hurriedly, and the fourth almost not at all. I sat through many of the negotiations meetings—sometimes as an official delegate of Uganda and sometimes as a civil society representative. I can say with some authority that the EC had no intention of helping the ACP countries go on with regional consultations. For some time, the ACP countries did maintain their unity and solidarity, but as time went on, the EC was able to fragment them. Europe did not want to negotiate with the ACP as a bloc. Later, when it came to negotiating with African, Caribbean, and Pacific countries separately, it became apparent that the EC was moving towards fragmenting them—in particular, Africa—even further. In the case of East Africa, for example, the EC exploited the distinction between Kenya and the other countries in the region. Kenya was the only non-LDC country, and therefore not eligible for the LDC system of WTO preferences, so the EC dealt with Kenya separately. This is how the REPA of the original Cotonou Agreement became simply EPA. The 'R' disappeared almost surreptitiously.

As for capacity building, I will give a small illustration. On 3 June 2001, at a meeting (at which I was present), the chairman of the ACP Trade Committee reported that there was slippage in implementation of regional seminars, and analytical studies were delayed because of a delay in the release of funds by the EC—funds that were pledged under the Cotonou Agreement. This happened frequently. The EC held the purse string and it did not release the money it had committed to releasing. As indicated earlier, the ACP ambassadors work out of the ACP House in Brussels, owned by the EC. They depend on EC largesse and per diems to attend meetings and conferences. With such a degree of dependence on EC funds, it was hopelessly naïve to assume that the EC would go out of its way to finance regional seminars and analytical studies.

Everything was stacked against the ACP and in favour of the EC. The EC decided the pace of the negotiations, the agenda, the preparations leading up to the negotiations and the text to be negotiated. It was the EC that produced the text every time, and the ACP ambassadors had to either sign on the dotted line or negotiate. The EC was always in a hurry to get on to phases II and III. The EC bureaucracy was under increasing pressure from lobbying groups (such as, for example, the food industry and the pharmaceutical companies), and so was always in too much of a rush to get things stitched up. The result was that the ACP countries were never able to reach their ambitions of regional integration, or for that matter a studied analysis of complex issues presented by the EC. For many ACP embassies, the staff turnover was frequent and capricious. And so when the EC deftly dropped the 'R' in the REPA concept, nobody in Africa even noticed, and soon the negotiations were about the EPAs. In the end, Africa was so divided that the EC started negotiating with individual countries, dictated by the whims of the EC bureaucracy in Brussels rather than by the development or welfare needs of the people of Africa.

So over time—like a distorting mirror—the REPA became the EPA, then the EPA became the IEPA, then the FEPA, then the CEPA, and so on ('I' is Interim; 'F' is Framework; and 'C' is Comprehensive). The core 'EPA' remained, and although nobody talked about it, the 'EPA' had in fact become 'NEPA' (National EPA), for the EC had effectively been signing separate national EPAs with individual African countries.

How the People of East Africa Trounced the European Commission
Dar es Salaam

As President Jakaya Kikwete entered the state lounge where President Mkapa and I were waiting for him on the warm, steamy day of 3 June 2010, he greeted Mkapa with a traditional welcoming 'Shikamu!' Twelve years younger than Benjamin Mkapa, Kikwete had worked in Mkapa's cabinet, first as Finance Minister and then as Minister of Foreign Affairs. In 2005, he had succeeded Mkapa as President of Tanzania. Turning to me, Kikwete reminded me that I was his 'Mwalimu' (teacher) some thirty years ago at the University of Dar es Salaam. After I took in this rather unexpected recognition, I quickly got down to the business at hand. And the business was how to persuade President Kikwete, and through him the leaders of the East African Community (EAC), to *not* sign the Framework Economic Partnership Agreement (FEPA). This agreement would have been disastrous for Tanzania, for the EAC, and for Africa.

Tanzania had already signed the Interim agreement (IEPA) in 2009, and the European Commission fully expected the EAC to sign the FEPA. The FEPA was expected to be signed in five days, on 8 June. The FEPA was then expected to lead to the signing of a Comprehensive EPA (CEPA). Benjamin Mkapa, well versed in the intricacies of the EPA negotiations, left it for me to explain the purpose of our meeting. Armed with technical papers on the subject prepared by Aileen Kwa and her team of trade experts at the South Centre—among them Peter Lunenborg and Wase Musonge—I set about, in the limited time the President had, explaining why neither Tanzania nor the EAC should sign the FEPA.

The South Centre had drawn up a list of twenty-one issues. I had worked through them the previous night and reduced these to the seven most significant ones. I list them below. They show how the EC was driving the EAC agenda and trying to oblige the region to sign an agreement that was not only one-sided and unfair, but also went far beyond the remit of the WTO. I might add that although some of the language is 'technical,' its economic and political significance is not too difficult to comprehend.

As I was explaining each issue to the President, his two secretarial assistants took notes. The President asked for further elaboration on the issues and the strategy the ECA might follow. It was

---

The seven most contentious issues in the EC-proposed text to the EAC on FEPA

1. FEPA demanded 80 percent tariff liberalisation from EAC. This would open EAC market to a flood of foreign imports that would kill whatever industries the EAC had locally and cause massive unemployment.
2. FEPA allowed only 17.4 percent of value of imports from Europe as sensitive products to the EAC. This was not enough. To have a dynamic trade policy that supports industrialisation, the EAC should have the flexibility to protect its production potential over the long term.
3. The EU had not made any real cuts to their food subsidies, and was not likely to in the future because of domestic political reasons. Hence, under FEPA they could bring subsidised food into the East African region, and threaten the region's food-based industries and long-term food security.
4. The Standstill Clause under FEPA (Art 13) forbade the EAC to increase tariffs during twenty-five years of liberalisation. It would foreclose the use of tariffs to protect East African industries in the future, and, in any case, it was incompatible with GATT Art 24.
5. Article 15 of FEPA disallowed new export taxes, or made them difficult to apply. This policy limitation was incompatible with WTO rules. More importantly, the EAC needed export taxes to preserve its natural resources for its own future industrialisation.
6. The MFN clause (Article 16) of the FEPA demanded that any concession the EAC made to, for example, China, India or Brazil, would have to be extended also to Europe. This would effectively undermine East Africa's efforts to build South-South relations.

---

not difficult to persuade the President that the EAC must remain united, and not allow the EC to divide the region by playing the 'non-LDC card' against Kenya. Under the WTO, the LDCs were exempt from tariff reduction commitments, but not Kenya. We ended our conversation with assurance from President Kikwete that he would not be party to this divide-and-rule tactic of the EC. It was time for press photographs and for Ben Mkapa and me to take our leave.

As I boarded the plane for Kampala I was mulling over my conversation with President Kikwete, and how a mere talk from me could counter the effect of development aid from Europe to Tanzania and East Africa—how to urge African policy makers to get out of this aid dependence that compromises sovereign policy making? How might East Africa resist signing an EPA with the European Union even if it meant losing development aid?[49] Would the double bind of the structural reality of aid dependence and the psychological dependency syndrome mean that my visit was foredoomed? If an individual at the summit of state power in Africa could overcome his or her own psychological dependency syndrome, could he or she then be able, also, to overcome the structural limitation? Do individuals in state power have any leverage that can overcome the structural bind? Or were they doomed in their structural bind to be forever servile? To put it in somewhat personal terms, would the confidence I placed in Kikwete's will (even if temporarily aroused) overcome the pessimism of my doubting spirit?

Kampala, Nairobi and Mombasa

Kampala was known for its seven magnificent hills (now many more) and the Makerere University is perched on one of them. I had taught at Makerere from 1964 to 1969, until Idi Amin's military coup had driven me to exile. After a beautiful ride from Entebbe airport next to Lake Victoria, I parked myself in a modest Kampala hotel. I was mandated by Ben Mkapa and Martin Khor (the Executive Director of the South Centre) to meet with President Yoweri Museveni. I knew him well from our past struggles against the dictatorship of Idi Amin (After the fall of Amin in 1979 we were in the same cabinet under President Binaisa). Museveni was widely recognised as a 'strong man,' with a quick-witted sharp mind that cuts through detail to get to the bigger issues—a man who took decisive action. It was important to get Museveni on our side. As it turned out, I could not meet him and so I wrote him a letter along the lines of my briefing to President Kikwete, hoping that he would (for old times' sake) take the time to read my letter. But I was taking no chances. I needed to involve Ugandan civil society in this effort to challenge the European Commission.

In 1998 I had come to Kampala to launch a branch of the Southern African Trade Information and Negotiations Institute (SEATINI), which I had founded in Zimbabwe the previous year. Its aim was (is) to help develop the capacity of trade officials in Southern and Eastern Africa to work towards a better deal for the region in the negotiations at the WTO and with the EU. One of the people in the audience at Makerere was Jane Nalunga, then holding a comfortable tenured post at the Bank of Uganda. Within months she left the post to help me set up the SEATINI office in Kampala and to run it as its Director. She has developed remarkable skills in putting across technical-cum-political arguments in a mellifluous, authoritative voice that cut through the jargon and got to the point. In 2004, she was joined by Nathan Irumba, one-time Ugandan Ambassador to Geneva, and a brilliant expert on trade issues. He became the Regional Director of SEATINI. In Nairobi, SEATINI was directed by Oduor O'ngwen, a veteran NGO and political activist.

854 million people today) despite commitments made at the 2000 Millennium Summit and the 2002 World Food Summit to halve it. Every five seconds, a child under 10 dies from hunger and malnutrition-related diseases. The situation, he said, is 'alarming.'[18]

Reasons behind the Worsening Food Security Situation in the Global South
Several reasons have contributed to the worsening food security situation in the Global South, among them:

- Global warming, which has disrupted the balance of natural systems of air, water and weather patterns essential for food production;
- Rising fuel prices, which pushes up the cost of, for example, fertilisers and transport;
- Land grabbing, in particular in Africa, by rich commercial farmers and global food corporations, disempowering small producers who are vulnerable to 'market attacks';
- The conversion of land for producing food into land for producing biofuels;
- The dismantling of the financial and physical infrastructure for rural agricultural: the removal of state subsidies for food production; the dismantling of village depots and local food reserves because of IMF-imposed Structural Adjustment Programmes (SAPs), which throw poor famers to the vagaries of the 'the market,' 'middle men,' and global seed and fertiliser corporations;[19]
- Financial speculation in the food sector;
- US and EU subsidies, including the practice of 'shifting boxes' (see below) in order to maintain subsidies, and EU Common Agricultural Policy (CAP) reform.

All these factors, and more, need to be recognised in order to comprehend the real reasons behind increasing impoverishment, malnutrition and misery, especially in rural areas of the Global South.

Significance of Agriculture in the WTO Agenda

We mentioned earlier that under the pre-WTO GATT, the US and the EU did not want agriculture in the multilateral trading system. Only when the US and EU (the developing countries were irrelevant) agreed to allow their respective trade-distorting subsidies to continue was agriculture brought under WTO discipline. Those subsidies still largely remain in place, and are at the core of the problem of the global malfunction of the agricultural system. Today, the US and EU use sophisticated linguistic distortions and euphemisms—such as the 'multifunctionality' of agriculture—to continue to protect their farmers and food corporations, which wield considerable clout in their 'democratic' political systems. The problem is political.

I shall deal with the question of the EU's Common Agricultural Policy (CAP) reform in the chapter on 'Europe's Trade War on Africa' (chapter three). Here I focus specifically on the issue of subsidies in the context of WTO negotiations, which is like walking through a minefield. The jargon of negotiations is very legalistic and technical, but I shall try to explain these in plain language.

The Shifting Boxes Phenomenon

I noted earlier that in the 1980s, European domestic and export subsidies resulted in large crop surpluses and downward pressure on food prices. Under the Agreement on Agriculture (AoA), all subsidies have to be reduced. There is a minimum allowed subsidy, called 'de minimis,' which is 5 percent of the value of production, or 10 percent in the case of developing countries. There is also an upper limit, called 'aggregate measurement of support' (AMS). The subsidies are classified into different categories (or 'boxes') depending on their effect on production and trade. *Amber* subsidies are directly linked to production levels, and are limited; *blue* subsidies are production-limiting subsidies that still distort trade, and have to be reduced over time; and *green* subsidies are supposed to cause minimal distortion, but they must be provided through a government-funded programme that does not involve transfers from consumers or price support to producers.

These provisions were worked out mostly by the Global North during the Uruguay Round, and they function asymmetrically, to the disadvantage of developing countries. But even within Northern countries, they disadvantage smaller farmers. Overall production levels in the US and Europe are so high that even the *de minimis* support runs to billions of dollars every year. According to the World Bank, Europe and the US spend $380 billion every year on agricultural subsidies alone. More than half of the EU's support goes to only 1 percent of producers—the giant food corporations; in the US, 70 percent of subsidies go to 10 percent of producers, also the larger agribusinesses.[20]

The effect of these subsidies is to flood global markets with below-cost commodities, depressing prices and undercutting producers in poor countries. The US Farm Bill has programmes which target eight crops, all sensitive for developing countries: cotton, wheat, corn, soybeans, rice, barley, oats, and sorghum. The impact on African countries has been particularly severe—production has fallen across many countries and in many cases small farmers that grew cereal, cotton, poultry and dairy have gone out of business.

The developed countries have used sophisticated policy tools to switch from amber and blue boxes to green boxes. Thus, for example, between 1995 and 2009 the EU cut down its amber box tariffs from €50,181 million to €8,764 million, and its blue box tariffs from €20,846 to €5,324. But, at the same time, it raised its green box tariffs from €18,779 million to €63,798 million.[21]

This shifting boxes phenomenon has undermined the very spirit of the Uruguay Round agreements. By contrast, African countries, for example, have been obliged under the WTO and bilateral trade agreements with Europe to cut down their 'applied

EU DOMESTIC SUPPORT (BASED ON WTO NOTIFICATIONS

Figures in millions of euros

Marketing year starting in	Total Amber	Total Blue	Total de minimis	OTDS	Total Green	Total domestic support
1995	50,181	20,846	825	71,852	18,779	90,631
1996	51,163	21,521	761	73,445	22,130	95,576
1997	50,346	20,443	733	71,521	18,167	89,688
1998	46,947	20,504	525	67,975	19,168	87,143
1999	48,157	19,792	554	68,502	21,916	90,419
2000	43,909	22,223	745	66,876	21,848	88,724
2001	39,391	23,726	1,012	64,128	20,661	84,790
2002	28,598	24,727	1,942	55,266	20,404	75,670
2003	30,891	24,782	1,954	57,626	22,074	79,700
2004	31,214	27,237	2,042	60,493	24,391	84,884
2005	28,427	13,445	1,251	43,123	40,280	83,404
2006	26,632	5,697	1,975	34,304	56,530	90,833
2007	12,354	5,166	2,389	19,909	62,610	82,519
2008	11,796	5,348	1,083	18,226	62,825	81,051
2009	8,764	5,324	1,402	15,489	63,798	79,288

I mention SEATINI because NGOs, and the people working in them, matter. There is a common misunderstanding that NGOs are just 'talk shops.' This perception is too one-sided and biased. SEATINI is only one among many NGOs in the region (and in Africa) that has been protecting the interests of ordinary people when their governments are too weak to stand up to the dictates of the Empire. Another one is the Kenya Human Rights Commission (KHRC). It had produced papers on the Legal Implications of the EAC-FEPA, urging leaders in East Africa not to trade the lives of our people with Europe.[50] There were several other NGOs working against the European efforts to impose a FEPA on the people of East Africa. I might add that in Europe too there are some strong NGO solidarity activists who have been very helpful in the struggle against the EPAs—among them, to mention a few, the Brussels-based Coalition of Flemish North-South Movement's 11.11.11; activists like Marc Maes; the European APRODEV network activists like Karin Ulmer; and the Africa programme of the Rosa Luxemburg Foundation (Berlin).

Already in preparation for the expected European 'attack' on the FEPA front, SEATINI had organised several meetings with various stakeholders—including government officials, the private sector, members of national and East African Community parliaments, other civil society organisations, and the media—ventilating their concerns about the FEPA. Now, at this point, the role of the East African Legislative Assembly (EALA) was going to be crucial. The NGOs decided to 'target' the EALA members of parliament. They were up against not only the powerful and well-resourced European Commission but also the EAC Secretariat at Arusha—an organ of the Community that should have been protecting the EAC but appeared to be siding with the EC. Already, the EC had penetrated the EAC bureaucracy in Arusha in a bid to prepare the ground for the signing of the FEPA. On 9 June, 2010, the EAC Secretariat and the EC had issued a joint Communiqué saying that the FEPA was ready for signature at a meeting in Dar es Salaam as a step towards signing a CEPA by the end of November, 2010.

The two organs of the community—the Secretariat and EALA—had different views, not only on the EPAs but also on the critical issue of securing funds from the EC to finance their activities. The Secretariat thought that the talks had dragged on for years, and had to come to an end; the EALA was of the view that the EAC must not be rushed into signing a document pushed by the European Commission. Also, the EALA was opposed to being lured by the EC's largesse. At its meeting in Kigali in April 2011, for instance, the EALA had objected to the use of $3.48 million in grant money mobilised by the EAC secretariat from the Swedish International Development Agency (SIDA) to facilitate the EPA negotiations process. It argued that using a grant from SIDA to finance the talks would not only compromise negotiations to the partner states' detriment but would as well prejudice and weaken any stronger stance the latter may adopt on the negotiations.[51]

To counter this double onslaught—externally by the European Commission and internally by the EAC Secretariat— SEATINI had prepared a position paper which was later signed by a number of civil society organisations throughout East Africa. This was to play a crucial role in Mombasa and Dar es Salaam in the next few days. The first stop was Mombasa.

The East African legislative assembly meeting in Mombasa
One of the principal voices of the people in East Africa is that of the members of the East African Legislative Assembly (EALA). The EALA was set up under the treaty signed on 30 November 1999 by Uganda, Kenya, and Tanzania establishing the EAC. Burundi and

Rwanda acceded to the treaty on 18 June 2007. Under the treaty, the Assembly is comprised of: nine members elected by each Partner State, ex-officio members consisting of the Minister or Assistant Minister responsible for the EAC from each Partner State, and the Secretary General and the Counsel to the Community. Of its fifty-two members (in 2010), twenty are women—some of the most active defenders of the rights of the people of the region. The mission of the EALA is to legislate, do oversight, and represent the people of East Africa in a bid to foster economic, social, cultural, and political integration. The bills passed by the EALA, once assented to by the heads of state of the five countries, are binding on the five governments. It is thus, at least in theory, a 'supranational' legislative body of the EAC.

The EALA met in Mombasa in the first week of June 2010. By this time its members were inundated with several documents on FEPA. Among these was a letter to EAC trade ministers from their ambassadors in Geneva, and a number of briefing and advocacy papers from civil society groups, including the SEATINI-drafted statement signed by several NGOs—all of them trying to persuade the EAC not to sign the EC draft on FEPA. The NGO representatives—including Jane Nalunga, Oduor, and other NGO reps—placed themselves in the lobby of the hotel where the EALA members were staying. [52]

The outcome of all this collective effort was a carefully crafted resolution passed by the EALA on 3 June. It started with a strong political preamble that expressed the EAC's willingness to sign the FEPA, provided that it resolved a number of outstanding issues in line with a regional approach. Among the outstanding issues were a number of those listed in the box above. Unless these issues were properly resolved, the EALA resolution stated, the EPA framework would bind the EAC to poor trading terms. It said that the EAC was not competitive with the EU, and so imports from the EU could undermine the EAC's industrialisation, and that the EU's agricultural subsidies threatened EAC farmers, especially in dairy, and also jeopardised food security in the region. It warned the EAC negotiators that if not fairly negotiated, the EU's protectionist policies would expose the EAC to unfair trade incommensurate with development benchmarks. The resolution ended by urging the EAC Council of Ministers to delay the signing of FEPA, to revise it, and to bring it for parliamentary approval both in the Partner States and at the regional level.

The EALA resolution instructing the Council of Ministers to delay signing the FEPA until all controversial issues were resolved now suddenly became poignant; it acquired a new political weight. The EU delegation was in a quandary: what were they to do now? How were they to go around this uncomfortable and unexpected voice of the democratic structure of the EAC? Democracy is all fine, but not when it gets in the way of *BusinessEurope*, the corporate war council. Profits must come before democracy. I know from previous experience that whenever the Europeans have failed in the past to get their way because of obstruction from NGOs or nationalist politicians or state officials, they run to the ministers and even the heads of states to get over these 'democratic' hurdles from below. [53] So on this occasion, too, De Gucht thought that the EALA did not matter; he could reach President Kikwete, who was that year the Chairman of the EAC Summit. However, when De Gucht phoned the State House in Dar es Salaam to speak to President Kikwete, he was politely told that unfortunately the President was 'out of town.'

When I was told about this, I mused about my reflections following my discussion with President Kikwete in company with former President Mkapa: Do individuals in state power have any leverage that can overcome the structural bind? Or were they doomed in their structural bind to be forever servile? . . . Would the confidence I placed in Kikwete's will overcome the pessimism of my doubting spirit? It thrilled me that the President kept his promise.

The people, but above all the East African parliamentarians of the EALA, had won the day, at least in June 2010.

Kenya small-scale farmers challenge the state on EPAs

The stand that the EALA took against EPA, despite efforts by the EC Commission to undermine it, was, if you like, at the apex—i.e., at the legislative level, which government ministers could not ignore. But I should inform you also about the struggle of the people at the grassroots level.

Whilst African states and governments were still in the connivance/adaptation phase, the people at the grassroots were moving into the resistance phase. In 2007, the Kenya Small-Scale Farmers Forum (KSSFF) filed a case against the government of Kenya on the EPA issue. In their complaint the Forum argued that if the EPAs were signed in their current form, they would put at risk the livelihoods of millions of farmers across Kenya and the rest of the East African region. They might have added that the EPAs would also hold back Kenya and the region's industrialisation.

It took six years for the High Court of Kenya to come to a decision. On 30 October 2013, the High Court ruled in the farmer's favour. The Court also directed the government to establish a mechanism for involving stakeholders (including the small-scale farmers) in the ongoing EPA negotiations, and furthermore, to publish, within thirty days, information regarding the negotiations for public awareness and in order to encourage public debate on this matter of utmost importance to the people of Kenya.

On 20 September 2014, a story went around that the five members of the EAC had signed the EPA with Europe. Why, after nearly four years of successfully resisting pressure from the EU, would the EAC governments sign the agreement? What would they have gotten out of it?

Let us look at this a bit more closely. In an in-house brief prepared on 23 May 2013 for the Chairman of the South Centre—President Mkapa—its Secretariat showed that the assessed cost of signing the EPA would far outweigh the benefits. Here are some of the highlights of this brief:

1. The EAC's four members—Burundi, Rwanda, Tanzania, and Uganda—were LDCs (Least Developed Countries). Even if they did not sign the EPA, their trade with the EU would not be affected, as they would then still be able to have duty-free and quota-free access to the EU market under the EU's Everything but Arms (EBA) agreement.

2. The only country that would be affected was Kenya (a non-LDC). Under most-favoured-nation (MFN) terms, Kenya would face higher tariffs than the EU's GSP. But even then, it was mainly the flower industry that would be affected; when entering the EU, Kenyan flowers would face tariffs of between 8.5 percent and 12 percent. In aggregate, without the EPA, Kenya's exports to the EU would face duties of up to $97 million a year. The 'benefit' of the EPA was therefore $97 million a year. Against this, by signing the EPA, Kenya faced the prospect of losing revenue to the tune of $742 million a year by the end of the implementation period after twenty-four years, if import increases were taken into account.

3. The comparable revenue losses (assuming import increases) for the other four LDCs of the EAC, if they signed the agreement, were calculated as:

- $940 million per year for Tanzania
- $597 million per year for Uganda
- $241 million per year for Rwanda
- $24 million per year for Burundi

4. That was not the only loss. The signing of the EPA would jeopardise the livelihood of several million small farmers, poultry farmers, and fisher folk in East Africa. There was then the effect on the future prospect of industrialisation in East Africa. The South Centre argued that the EAC was more competitive than the EU on only 10 percent of total tariff lines. In other words, the EU could out-compete East African industries in their own backyard in 90 percent of their tariff lines. With the 82 percent tariff liberalisation that the EPA demanded, a total of 2,366 tariff lines would be liberalised, making the possibility of having future domestic production in these products questionable. A short list of sectors that could be affected by imports from Europe included the following:

- processed oil products;
- chemical products for agriculture;
- commodity chemicals;
- medicines, vaccines, and antibiotics;
- intermediate industrial products;
- final industrial products;
- vehicle industry;
- agricultural products; and
- books, brochures, and other printed material.

The South Centre brief concluded: 'The cost of the EPA for Tanzania and the EAC as a whole is therefore higher than its benefits.'

As against this assessment of the South Centre and other similar analysis by East Africa-based civil society organisations—such as SEATINI and the Kenya Human Rights Commission (KHRC)—there were no comparable comprehensive studies either from the relevant ministries of the East African governments or from the East African Secretariat in Arusha.

Nonetheless, just as the book was going to the press, the East African governments concluded the EPAs, pending signature. Given the above analysis of the South Centre and other civil society organisations that have an expertise on issues related to Africa's international trade, one is obliged to raise the question: Why would the governments of the East African Community want to conclude an agreement that is against the interest of their economies and of their people?

The answer to this will have to wait for a full disclosure of what took place behind the scene during the months preceding the signing—a task left to historians. At this time, based on my experience and knowledge of the principal actors in this 'war,' I can only offer areas where future historians might want to undertake more comprehensive research.

1. Increasing pressure from the European Union since its failure to get the EAC to sign the CEPA in November 2010. The EU issued what amounted to an ultimatum: if the EPA was not signed by 1 October 2014, East Africa would invite serious counter-action from the EU, which would hurt East African economies.[54]
2. Mounting pressure from the flower export industry in Kenya, an industry in the control of large global corporations as well as some wealthy and influential Kenyans.

3. The weakening of East African political leadership on the EPA issue. This could be a direct result of their dependence on 'development aid' money promised by Europe. In my earlier writings I have described the benefits of 'development aid' as illusory.[55]

4. The effect of the dependence of the EAC Secretariat on aid from the European Union. Slightly over 60 percent ($78.17 million) of the EAC budget for 2014–15 was funded by the donors, and 32 percent ($41.9 million) by the five EAC countries. There was also a modest $5.0 million from 'other agencies.' It was therefore not surprising that the EC saw the EAC Secretariat as its ally in hastening the process of signing the EPAs.

5. The weakening of the influence of the East African Legislative Assembly (EALA) and of civil society organisations on the course of EPA negotiations between 2010 and 2014.

6. An additional contributing factor was the new geopolitical global dynamics in which East Africa appears to have taken the side of Western countries—led by the US and Europe—against the increasing threat of 'Islamic terrorism.' There has been an appreciable increase in the military presence of the NATO countries in Africa (especially the US, Britain, and France) since the forcible removal from power of Libya's Gaddafi, and the mayhem in the Middle East and the Sahara region extending into Somalia. East African countries—especially Kenya and Uganda—received millions of dollars' worth of military hardware from the West between 2012 and 2014.

However, it is one thing to conclude an agreement, another to get it ratified by the respective national assemblies before it is implemented. There still remained a number of critical issues that were left unresolved—among them: the issue of export taxes (the EAC countries' right to impose levies on the export of commodities that they need for their own industrialisation); the issue of the 'Non-Execution Clause' (which permitted the European Commission to impose sanctions against EAC countries that fail to abide by the principles of humans rights, democracy and good governance); and the issue of the so-called 'Rendezvous Clause' consisting of matters such as investment, government procurement, competition policy and services.

And then there is the question of the implementation of the EPA, for it is one thing to sign an agreement and another to put it to action.

CONCLUSIONS

One: The experience of Africa in relation to Europe shows that trade is only a soft word for war. Europe's threat to impose sanctions as its final weapon of 'persuasion' in the EPA negotiations was an act of war. I will take this issue up again in chapter five, 'Trade Sanctions as Acts of War.'

Two: We are dealing here with embedded structures left behind in Africa by a hundred years of colonial rule. One would have thought that fifty years was enough to get rid of these structures. Asian countries have a better record in handling this problem than African. This may have to do with the quality of their leaders; but I believe that this has to do more with the geopolitics of the two regions.

Three: We must avoid a preordained conclusion (often from the left) that all efforts to work with the corrupt leadership of the neo-colonies are foredoomed. This is dogmatism. Pushed to its logical conclusion, this leads to a deterministic cul-de-sac: nothing can be done until there is an end to capitalism, or until there is a 'regime change' that brings into power 'revolutionary leadership.' That may be so, but until these happen, the structures of dependence can be broken, not necessarily in one fell swoop, but bit by bit, chip by chip.

I come back to this issue in chapter six, 'From War to Peace: The Theory and Practice of Revolutionary Change.'

Four: One of these 'chips' that can be broken is so-called 'development aid.' Institutionalised aid gets embedded into structures and habits that have a tendency to reproduce themselves. This is what has happened to the entire edifice of EPA negotiations. The ACP House in Brussels is more than an architectural expression of this edifice. It is an expression of a begging hand that tells the master, give me some money so I can study the situation in order to prepare myself to negotiate with you. It is the height of naivety. If you need to talk with your adversary, finance your own 'capacity building,' as it is known in the official jargon.

Five: The language of trade negotiations has to be deconstructed so that it makes sense to the ordinary citizen. These technical terms do not just drop from the sky. They have a history and a purpose to them. Abstracted from history, the jargon acquires a life of its own. Words become realities. We saw how the words 'preference' and 'preferential tariffs' came into the vocabulary of trade negotiations during colonial times as 'imperial preference,' and then evolved into something quite the opposite. What in reality was a 'preference' in favour of the Empire was presented as if it were a 'preference' in favour of the colonies. This linguistic twist and the use of colonial metaphors masks an oppressive and exploitative system. Understandably, technical jargon in relation to trade negotiation is unavoidable. But it is the task of trade negotiators from the countries of the South to flesh out its implications for state policies and the lives and jobs of ordinary people.

Going beyond words, it is even more important to seize the narrative. Colonial narratives persist. If you do not write your own story, others will write it for you. This book is about our side of the story as we narrate it.

4. TECHNOLOGY AND INTELLECTUAL PROPERTY WARS

One lethal weapon in the arsenal of the West's trade war against the Rest is intellectual property. The common heritage of humanity—including medical knowledge and the seeds for food—is turned into property under capitalism, to be bought and sold as 'IP.' This chapter is about the struggle in the various organs of global governance—including the WTO, the World Intellectual Property Organisation (WIPO), and the World Customs Organisation (WCO). It is also about technology and the efforts by Africa and the Third World to industrialise.

INTRODUCTION

It has been a well-recognised fact throughout written history that knowledge shared is knowledge multiplied. A physical commodity that is consumed becomes extinct. I consume an apple and it is no more. But knowledge is metaphysical. It is enriched when it is 'consumed' by an ever-expanding circle of consumers. Knowledge is turned into a 'commodity' for profit. [56]

During the 1980s and 1990s I worked in many countries in eastern and southern Africa, and then for four years at the South Centre—2005–09. I can say from my experience that the industrialised countries of the North have been trying systematically to block all efforts by the countries of the South to industrialise. Their mega-corporations have tried—and, alas, succeeded—in privatising knowledge, and using it to promote corporate profits over the lives of people. I give illustrative examples from the agricultural and the pharmaceutical sectors to show this.

In 2009, after I had finished my work at the South Centre, I was, for three months, a visiting professor at the University of Uppsala in Sweden. One day, a newspaper item caught my eye. It was a report about the conference of the Pirate Parties International (PPI) held in Uppsala. In their manifesto the PPI declared, among other things, that patents on life (including seeds and genes) should not be allowed. This is exactly what I was advocating in the 1980s and 1990s—nearly two decades earlier—whilst working in the rural areas of Southern Africa. Nobody had taken the slightest notice of what I was saying. So I was delighted that the youthful 'pirate' parties of Europe were getting their voices heard—although their aims and objectives were somewhat different from mine.[57] Since 2009, they have followed through their victory by securing electoral seats in European national parliaments. But, for us in the South, using knowledge encased in 'IP' regimes without paying enormous royalties to the 'owners' of this 'property' constitutes an act of 'piracy.' The war goes on.

It is the seeds and pharmaceutical companies of the West that have pirated the knowledge of seeds and medicinal products from the South. But whereas in the South this knowledge was shared as a public asset, the Western companies, having learnt from the South, proceeded to claim it as their private property. They are guilty—morally guilty—for the avoidable deaths of millions of people in the South who cannot afford their 'patented' medicines against, for example, AIDS, malaria, tuberculosis and other killer diseases. It is a sordid story. But it is not all doom and gloom. Those who control the system (the global corporations and the international organisations that the West controls) do not get their own way entirely. Wars do not always end in the victory of the militarily or 'intellectually' powerful.

INNOVATION, DEVELOPMENT, AND INTELLECTUAL PROPERTY
The Commodification of Knowledge is a Relatively Recent Phenomenon

The commodification of 'knowledge'—or, turning knowledge into the private property of global corporations—is a product of the emergence of capitalism in Europe. That was some five-hundred years ago. But even then it took a long time for it to be privatised—in fact, effectively not until the WIPO was created in 1967, less than fifty years ago. Why did it take such a long time? The reason is that for hundreds of years, the industrialising countries of the world were borrowing, poaching, copying and 'pirating' one another's innovations because they were preoccupied with their own industrialisation. It is only in the last hundred years that they have become property-conscious of their innovations. They still share knowledge among themselves through their globalised corporations. But now that the developing countries are beginning to challenge them, they have built protective ramparts around this 'property.' Europeans (and now Americans and the Japanese) claim that they have exclusive domain over innovation and technology on which they have put their 'intellectual' stamp. The Swiss, for example, developed their pharmaceutical industry through what today would be called 'piracy' under the WIPO—an organisation that, ironically, is now located in the Swiss capital.

Most people in the West do not know that 'European' science was built upon the foundation of ancient Egyptian, Meso-American, Chinese, Indian, Greek, Roman/Byzantine, and medieval Islamic sciences. The European medieval period (from about 500 to 1100 AD) is often described as the 'dark ages'—a setback from the more progressive antecedent periods of the Roman and Greek empires. When Enlightenment came to Europe it was as a result of complex processes, among them the freeing of the sciences from religion. Islamic science played a role in re-linking Europe with Greek classical writings, and with the sciences, during the period of the Enlightenment.[58] However, in our own times, because of institutionalised racism and Islamophobia, this part of history is generally lost to the younger generation. The youth in Europe believe that all modern science is a Western creation—that the North is the producer of knowledge and the South its consumer. This is what lies behind European narcissism and hubris.

The Berne Convention (1886) is often cited as the beginning of the IP system. But this is only partly true, and indeed only in a very small part. The convention was primarily aimed at protecting literary works, and was influenced by Victor Hugo and the French 'right of the author' (*droit d'auteur*). There was a lot of opposition to it. For example, the Dutch argued that it would stifle the Dutch printing industry. The UK signed it in 1887 but refused to implement large parts of it until the signing of the Copyright, Designs and Patents Act in 1988 (a hundred years later). The United States did not sign the Berne Convention until 1989.

The Myth of IP as Essential for Innovation and Development

So I am not taken in by the myth created by Western hegemonic ideologues about the necessity of 'intellectual property' for innovation and development. There is not the slightest evidence of this. In fact, IP regimes are major obstacles to the development of science and industry—especially in the South. The International Assessment of Agricultural Science and Technology (IAASTD)'s report—a work of four hundred scientific experts—criticised the present trade and IP regimes as favouring the rich countries at the cost of the poor. It said that IP as applied to the protection of genetically modified organisms (GMOs) has affected public research and farmers' rights to seeds.[59] Also, the World Health Organisation's Consultative Expert Working Group (CEWG) on Research and Development issued a report along similar lines on the issue of research and development (R&D) on health and medicines.[60] In its report, the CEWG recommended open approaches to R&D and innovation and the adoption of a binding convention that guarantees that the results of R&D will be a public good, i.e., not subject to appropriation but free for use, to generate medicines needed particularly in developing countries.

Are Developing Countries Right in Supporting the IP System?

Nowadays we hear a new argument coming from the newly industrialising countries (NICs) of the South. They say that they are not necessarily opposed to the IP system; they are opposed to its monopolisation by the West. They want room to develop their own innovations and IP regimes.

Let us consider this for a moment. There is something wrong about this position too. I acknowledge that there are two sides to this argument, but I still hold that the whole system of privatising what should be part of public knowledge (part of 'the commons') is wrong and unjustified.

From the perspective of the NICs, and given the wide gap between them and Western industrialised countries, this is perhaps understandable. The present system of monopoly control over industrial knowledge (by most accounts, the developed countries hold about 95 percent of all patents worldwide) inhibits their ability to industrialise; it is one of the main reasons for the delayed or retarded industrialisation of the South. There is a very high cost to transferring IP from the North to the South. For example,

China is developing into the manufacturing center of the world in our times. However, it is not generally known that China pays a heavy price for the transfer of technology. It pays more than $4 billion each year for patents alone. In some cases, for example DVD machines, Chinese companies pay more than $30 as royalty fees for each machine, whilst the Chinese manufacturers get only $2.[61]

Faced by this situation, not only China but also other countries in Asia, Africa, and Latin America are engaged in the 'piracy' of intellectual property. They have become targets of the developed countries. The Western countries have set up an elaborate system of surveillance against the South for what they call 'industrial espionage,' even as, paradoxically, they steal and pirate from one another as well.[62] The IP anti-counterfeiting and enforcement agenda involves hundreds of OECD-based global businesses and their foreign subsidiaries, such as the US Chamber of Commerce's 'Coalition against Counterfeiting and Piracy Intellectual Property Enforcement Initiative: Campaign to Protect America,' and the Security and Prosperity Partnership of North America. Having failed to impose civil remedies through local courts, the North is looking at criminalising and internationalising IP violations, and widening the scope of enforcement through such organisations as the World Health Organisation, especially its International Medical Products Anti-Counterfeit Taskforce (IMPACT), WIPO's Advisory Committee on Enforcement (ACE), the Anti-Counterfeiting Trade Agreement (ACTA), Standards to be Employed by Customs for Uniform Rights Enforcement, (SECURE), and Interpol.

The Western countries are using IP agreements, bilateral and regional free trade agreements, investment treaties, and Economic Partnership Agreements (EPAs) to advance their economic interests. For example, Article 11D of the 1996 IP agreement between the US and Cambodia limited Cambodia's flexibility with regard to its *sui generis* system for plant protection. The Cotonou Agreement between the European Union and Africa includes patenting for biotechnology inventions and plant varieties and legal protection for databases.

So, yes, there is a good case to be made in defence of the developing countries defying the IP regimes enforced by the West and Western-dominated international organisations. It is clear that as long as capitalism remains the dominant system of global production and exchange, it would be wrong to deny the countries of the South the ability to take protective measures against the North. The North's monopolised knowledge is unacceptable. The criminalisation of the spread of industrial knowledge and the vast system of global espionage that it has generated are not only wasteful of resources; they also created a 'global police state,' an Orwellian world.[63]

Notwithstanding my support for defensive action by developing countries under the present circumstances, I would still insist that the whole system of privatising industrial knowledge is wrong. There was a time when the transfer of technology took place on the basis of solidarity rather than royalties. Following the 1939–45 Second Imperial War, the Soviet Union transferred vast amounts of industrial knowledge not only within the Soviet bloc, but also to countries like China and India. Some more recent developments augur well for the future. Transfers of knowledge take place these days, also, using so-called 'open source' technologies, which do not carry copyright licenses.[64] Furthermore, civil society activists are increasingly taking a stand against the monopolisation of knowledge. In 2012 the US Congress was obliged to withdraw two proposed legislative measures that would have given authority to the government to block access to foreign websites on the grounds of copyright infringement. On one single day, 18 January 2012, 10 million petitions were signed against those bills—the Stop Online Piracy Act (SOPA) and the Protect Intellectual Property Act (PIPA).

Oppose the IP System but Choose your Technology

IP ideologues sometimes argue that those who are against IP are against technology, that they are present-day Luddites.[65] This is a diversionary tactic. I am opposed to the IP regime—that is, the conversion of technology into private property to earn 'rentier income' for those who claim to 'own' it. I am not against innovation or technology as such. Society cannot 'develop' without innovation. On the other hand, not all technologies are developmental; some are counter-developmental. If a certain technology harms human health or the environment, for example, then it is counter-developmental in the sense that I use the term. In some circumstances, I would even support going back to the 'old technology.' For example, Gandhi's use of the *charkha* to produce locally spun cloth (*khadi*) was neither Luddite nor atavistic but a smart political action against British rule.[66] In the same vein, I would argue that using 'indigenous' seeds, as opposed to genetically modified seeds, is not atavistic; it is a correct action against the domination of seed monopolies.

On this issue, as on many issues, I believe that the *precautionary principle* is a reasonable guide to action. This principle states that if there is a risk that an action or policy might cause harm to the public or to the environment, then, in the absence of scientific evidence, it is prudent to exercise caution. In the case of hybrid seeds, it is no longer a question of an absence of scientific evidence. There is ample evidence showing that the lives of millions are at risk in order to maximise profits for global mega-seed monopolies.

It is important to make a distinction between technology and innovation on the one hand, and the IP system on the other.

The two are not the same at all, although ideologues of the IP system would like us to believe that one (innovation) is not possible or feasible without the other (IP).

TECHNOLOGY WARS: THE CASE OF AGRICULTURAL SEEDS
A Hybrid Seed is Technology

There is one thing about seeds that is not so easy to grasp: a hybrid seed is technology.

I never fully understood this until I was doing research on maize in the Moshi-Arusha region whilst teaching at the University of Dar es Salaam in the 1970s. In 1975 Tanzania faced serious food shortages. Some observers blamed Nyerere's forced villagisation programme for the food shortages. But the experts I consulted during my research told me that there were two main reasons: one was the severe drought during the 1973–75 seasons, and the second was that Tanzania was using low-yielding local seeds. Until then most farmers used seeds saved from the previous year's harvest, but some middle-sized farms also used the improved open-pollinated varieties (OPVs) that were locally developed. They said that Tanzania needed to shift from local maize to hybrids.

Some fifteen years later, in 1990, I visited the region. Most small farmers still used their local varieties. They could not afford to buy the hybrids. Some also used the hybrid CG4141 seeds. After market liberalisation, foreign companies had come in to market their seeds. CG4141, marketed by Cargill (a global conglomerate), competed aggressively with the locally bred cultivars multiplied and sold by Tanseed (Tanzania Seed Company). CG4141 seed is 'improved' technology. I was told that the famers preferred CG4141 because of its higher yield, except that it was expensive, needed more water and fertilisers, and did not store as well as their old seeds. Also, the *ugali* (pounded maize cooked into dough) made from it was not as sweet as the old maize. But Tanseed did not have the financial muscle of Cargill. Cargill was winning, but the farmers were going into debt. CG4141 had embedded intellectual property rights owned by Cargill. Cargill extracted hefty royalties for the use of its seeds.

Traditional Knowledge: is it Superior to Modern Knowledge?

I also visited two villages in south-western Tanzania—Ukwile and Msia. At both villages people were engaged in Low External Input Agriculture (LEIA)—agricultural practices aimed at maximising the use of local knowledge and resources, and minimising the use of external inputs. People were experimenting with the use of *utupa* (*Trifosea Vogelli*)—a local tree known to the people as a pesticide for controling pests in maize production and storage. People in the area have traditionally used leaves from this tree and made them into a liquid solution for application to the crops. The people were experimenting with converting the leaves into a powder form, since it is easier to store the pesticides in dust form. They also planted *acacia albida* (a local tree) and sun hemp to fix nitrogen in the soil, and they planted indigenous varieties of trees and bushes (eg *nzigati*). The traditional knowledge of these was dying out.

Local *nganga*[67] and older people were consulted to identify these trees, and knowledge was resurrected for growing and duplicating these indigenous varieties. I attended one of their workshops where the nganga were telling the poor peasants to value their traditional knowledge. The following is an account from my notes taken at the workshop. 'Agriculture,' the nganga argued, 'is not just about obtaining high yields. It is also about conserving the soil. Soil consists of two distinct layers: topsoil humus that supports microbes and higher plant and animal life,

and a surface layer of almost lifeless bedrock.' The peasants nod-
ded in agreement, they knew all this already. 'But what is wrong
with applying fertilisers to the soil?' they asked. 'Fertilisers,' the
nganga explained, 'cause microbes to grow. These microbes feed
on humus, breaking it down faster than otherwise, thus enabling
the crops to grow faster also.' A villager got up and asked, 'What's
wrong with that?' The nganga explains, 'With no humus to hold
the soil, it gets washed away, and you have to use more and more
fertilisers to give the soil artificial nutrients, and the cycle continues. The energy cost of a unit of food thus goes up. Yes, you get
more yields per acre of land, but more and more of it goes to the
companies to pay for the fertilisers. So you may grow more and
earn less. You are now working for the corporations. That is the
immediate effect. But the more important long-term effect is that
you have lost control over your soil. The land may belong to you,
but that soil is no longer yours.' I listened in wonderment at the
knowledge of the nganga.

But the *nganga* were not having an easy time. Arraigned
against them were three forces. One consisted of EU-funded
NGOs such as Global 2000, which were distributing fertilisers free
of charge to the farmers. Secondly, there was pressure from the
better-off 'progressive' farmers who were boasting of their 'high
yields' using hybrids. And third, there was pressure from state
agricultural experts, who preached the value of High External
Input Agriculture (HEIA). The nganga needed time to show the
results of LEIA, but people were told that there was no time:
'development' means high yields and fast results. It seemed to me
that they were in a hurry, as if to catch a train to some urgent destination. In actual fact, these were 'negative' forces at work which
found the 'alternative' model of development a threat to their
interests.

It is a battle. The corporations play out their macabre war dance on the soil of Africa. They are aided by state agents and Western donor agencies pushing fertilisers and pesticides on the people to 'hurry, hurry, hurry' to some dubious destination called 'growth,' and the ordinary people (the more enlightened among them) urge the rest to pause and reflect on what they are doing and where they thought they were going.

Monsanto

The most attractive aspect of hybrids is their high yields. Their most destructive aspect is that they wipe out poor farmers who cannot afford the high cost of their production. Seed is only part of a bigger picture. It has to do with the control of not only food production but also of fertilisers, pesticides, herbicides, tube wells and mechanical agricultural tools such as tractors and combine harvesters. So, really, it is a veritable condition of war between big capital on one side and poor farmers on the other.[68] So on one side are millions of poor farmers and on the other is a highly concentrated group of global corporations that control genetically engineered seeds and chemicals. The biggest one is Monsanto. It did not start as a seed producer; it started out as a chemical company, and as the following diagram shows, it has 'cross-licensing' agreements with a number of chemical companies that produce various kinds of toxins (poisons).

In 2005 Monsanto filed a patent application for breeding techniques for pigs. This was contested by Greenpeace, who argued that Monsanto was trying to claim ownership on ordinary breeding techniques. In February 2012, two NGOs—Navdanya and No Patent on Seeds—filed a complaint against Monsanto claiming that virus-resistant melons were pirated by Monsanto from India. I realise that there are always two sides to a story, and

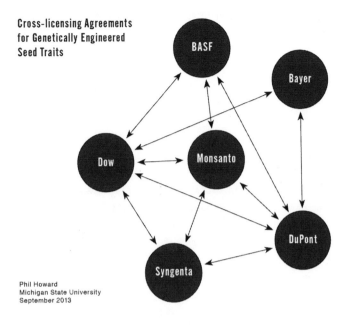

Cross-licensing Agreements for Genetically Engineered Seed Traits

Phil Howard
Michigan State University
September 2013

Monsanto and its well-paid lawyers have their own narrative. All the same, the above is enough to illustrate the ongoing battles between what is owned by the people (pig-rearing techniques in Europe and melons in India), and the appropriation of this pre-existing knowledge by the likes of Monsanto. The story does not end here. On 25 May 2013, there were worldwide protests against Monsanto in 436 cities and fifty-two countries. The Associated Press estimated that there were two million protestors.[69] In an earlier chapter on the WTO, we saw that the EU and the US spend billions every year on agricultural subsidies to support their farmers. If you think about it, it is clear that these subsidies actually go to enrich the Monsantos of this world that produce seed, fertilisers, and agricultural machinery. I also recounted the story of millions of cotton farmers in the four African states of Benin, Burkina Faso, Chad and Mali, who were literally ruined as a direct outcome of US subsidies to its cotton producers. These subsidies eventually go into the coffers of Monsanto, among other large corporations. This is not all. Having acquired patent rights on its seeds, Monsanto then takes ordinary farmers to court for patent infringement. In a report, the Center for Food Safety said that it discovered 142 patent infringement suits against 410 farmers and fifty-six small businesses in more than twenty-seven states as of December 2012. The amount of money pocketed by Monsanto comes to a whopping $23 million. The study was co-authored by the Save our Seeds (SOS) campaign.[70] Monsanto had developed what is colloquially known as 'terminator seeds.' Once these get into the soil they suicide (self-destroy) so the farmer has to buy new ones the year after.

If this is not war, what is?

My Experience in the Zambezi Valley of Zimbabwe

I will relate one more episode from my experience in Zimbabwe in the 1980s and 1990s. At the time I was working as a rural development 'expert' in north Zimbabwe, near the border with Zambia—an area called Lower Guruve, because it is on the lower part of a thousand-meter escarpment that separates the Zambezi Valley from the rest of Zimbabwe. Human settlements have existed around the relatively fertile areas below the escarpment and along the valleys and rivers flowing through the area, right up to the mighty River Zambezi that runs through Mozambique, Zambia, and Zimbabwe. The colonial government had damned the Zambezi River, creating one of the world's largest artificial lakes, Lake Kariba. Traditionally, people had lived off the resources of the river and the forest. There was plenty of food. People lived off fish, kudus, buffaloes and other wildlife and fruits. But after the dam was built, they were uprooted and removed from around the lake and pushed further south towards the escarpment. They were thus denied access to fish and wildlife—physically and by law. These were now reserved for tourists from the West who came to the Zambezi for fishing and hunting. This earned handsome revenues for the colonial state and the tour operators, but it impoverished the people. In the 1980s, as a result of migration from the Upper Guruve areas, the valley's resources faced serious stress. When I arrived in the area in the mid-1980s the people were struggling for basic survival. I saw massive deforestation as well as 'illegal' hunting and fishing. There was also tension between the autochthonous tribes and the migrants from above the escarpment.

This stressed land's natural environment (high temperatures—above 25 degrees centigrade—and rainfall below 600 mm annually) was tolerable for local grains (like millet and sorghum), wildlife, fish, and subtropical fruits. But successive governments (both colonial and postcolonial) introduced maize, cotton, and cattle. To make this possible they provided 'inducements' to attract foreign capital into the area, to enable hybrid maize and cotton. They also brought massive amounts of pesticides in order to get rid of the tsetse flies and enable cattle ranching. One does not have to be Einstein to understand that this was exactly the wrong thing to do in the valley.

The Swiss company Ciba Geigy (now part of Novartis) brought their hybrid maize and cotton into the valley. I used to visit the farms where these were being 'forcibly' grown—forcibly because production was 'induced' through huge amounts of fertilisers, pesticides and herbicides. Upon entering these farms we would be welcomed by Ciba Geigy and so-called 'extension experts' the Ministry of Agriculture sent there to 'teach' the 'ignorant' peasant farmers how to grow maize and cotton. We were each given a cap emblazoned with the words '*Kohwa Pakuru,*' meaning, literally, 'reap big' or 'increased harvest.' So, once again, what mattered were higher yields, not the cost of production or the lives of the people.

What was I to do as a rural development 'expert' in this situation? I was hired as a 'consultant' by the Lutheran World Federation. I took time to study the situation. Soon I found allies where, because of my ignorance, I had least expected them. When the British colonised the area in the 1890s, they had (as elsewhere in Africa) systematically destroyed the indigenous structures of political authority. The chiefs who had this authority by virtue of their royal lineage were forced to become salaried 'civil servants.' Those who resisted (like Chief Mzarabani in the valley) were demoted or thrown out, and new ones put in their place. These colonial chiefs were then engaged to collect taxes and organise forced-labour gangs for the British. They even lost their power to distribute land. These 'forced collaborators' thus lost their legitimacy in the eyes of the people.

However, I discovered something very interesting. The old chiefs never really 'died'; upon physical death, they became 'royal ancestors' (*mhondoro*), and communicated with the people through 'spirit mediums.' The most famous was the medium Mbuya Nehanda, who was among the leadership during the First *Chimurenga* War against the British in the 1890s, until she was caught and executed. Throughout British rule, and subsequently under the rule of the settlers (under Smith), hundreds of spirit mediums thus sustained the continued resistance against British conquest. Mbuya Nehanda's spirit provided the inspiration behind the Second Chimurenga War in the 1970s. The spirit mediums in the 1970s guided the liberation movement guerrillas through the forests and mountains of the Zambezi Valley. The chiefs (specially installed by the Smith government) were discredited, but not the spirit mediums. They lived rigorously abstemious lives—in their dress, in their relations with the opposite sex, and above all, in their abstention from the use of Western artefacts, including Western medicines. It is the last that caught my imagination.

The spirit mediums became my allies in fighting against Ciba Geigy and the 'extension experts' of the Ministry of Agriculture. They cautioned people against using fertilisers because, they argued, this would 'poison your soil and you won't be able to grow millet and sorghum.' They cautioned against the use of pesticides because these would 'kill the tsetse.' At first it was difficult for me to understand the logic behind this tsetse argument. Surely, I suggested, tsetse killed people. But the spirit mediums explained to me that the people had lived with the tsetse and the wildlife for a thousand years. More importantly, the tsetse infected only cattle, not wildlife. The environment was suited for the wildlife, not cattle. People knew how to hunt deer and kudus and live off wildlife, but the cattle that were brought into the valley from above the escarpment needed grazing land, which added to the deforestation that was already taking place. The cattle had to be protected from the tsetse with massive amounts of pesticides, which also poisoned the forest and the fruits of the valley. It made perfect sense to me that the tsetse flies were 'friends of the people.' Soon, we formed a group in order to launch a 'Save our Tsetse Flies' campaign. During those years (the 1980s) I also worked in South Matabeleland with a grassroots organisation—the Organisation of Rural Associations for Progress. Through them I learnt about Project CAMPFIRE—Communal Areas Management Programme for Indigenous Resources. This project was the inspiration behind the formation of the Lower Guruve Development Association, and the people of Lower Guruve, led by women, had begun to make progress towards providing an alternative to the Ciba Geigy model for the management of natural resources in the region. But the Save our Tsetse campaign never got off the ground because of logistical and political difficulties.

In the early 1990s, the government of Zimbabwe, pushed by the IMF and the World Bank, introduced a Structural Adjustment Programme. This was the final capitulation by the state to the dictates of global corporate capital. The spirit mediums in the valley, who had contributed so much to the liberation struggle, were disappointed. To my dismay I learnt—as I did in relation to my own country, Uganda—that political freedom did not necessarily translate into economic liberation or social justice. What surprised me was how quickly the new Zimbabwe government handed over the economy to the global corporate giants. In 1994 I decided to quit working as 'rural development expert,' and turned my energy to fighting the IMF, the World Bank, and the newly created WTO.

IP WARS: THE CASE OF THE PHARMACEUTICAL INDUSTRY

The IP system privileges the rich corporations at the cost of the lives of the poor. The poor cannot afford their expensive drugs. The pharmaceutical companies argue that their high prices cover their R&D costs. But if you go into this argument deeply, you will see that the companies simplify, to their own benefit, a very complex phenomenon.

Learning from African Experiences

When I used to work in the rural areas of Southern Africa in the 1980s, I often met with members of the Zimbabwe National Traditional Healers Association (ZINATHA). It was headed at the time by Professor Gordon Chavanduka, who told me that the association had some 80,000 members, working in areas where

Western-trained doctors never set foot. The traditional healers had a vast knowledge of herbs and medicines. He himself was often approached by drug companies. During my visits to villages, I used to accidentally come across agents of Western pharmaceutical companies in white overalls with syringes and other devices. They were collecting herbal samples and also blood samples from the villagers. They were also talking with the ZINATHA practitioners. Upon inquiring I found that they were working on antiretroviral drugs for HIV/AIDS. I suppose that when Novartis or GlaxoSmithKline or Pfizer come to Africa, they must build their travel costs, per diems, and much else besides into their 'R&D costs.' They took away herbal samples for free, got free advice from the ZINATHA members, and got free blood samples 'in the interest of science.'

My peripatetic research and development work took me to other parts of eastern and southern Africa besides Zimbabwe. My job was to spread the experience of communities in the region who were experimenting with alternative traditional knowledge that was in many instances superior to 'modern scientific' knowledge (see above about the nganga in the two villages in south-western Tanzania and their scientific knowledge of seeds and agriculture that was far superior to that of global agricultural corporations). In the mid-1980s my work took me to Botswana. I worked with an organisation called Thusano Lefatsheng, formed in 1984 by a group of women faced with the perennial problem of food security. They were engaged in harvesting their traditional knowledge about veld products, specifically indigenous food and medicinal plants such as Morula fruit and kernels, Morama tubers and beans, the Kalahari Devil's Claw plant (a well-known medicinal plant) and others. Around these indigenous crops, the women organised a range of activities, including production, harvesting, purchasing, processing, marketing, healing and other community activities.

I asked the women if they had visitors from outside. They said they were often visited by NGOs and donor organisations, and yes, sometimes 'white' people came to take samples of their herbal and medicinal plants.

TRIPS and the Production of Local Generics

I cite the above example not to dismiss the R&D work the pharmaceutical companies do but to show that they vastly exaggerate their importance, and more importantly, they do not own up to the debt they owe to, for example, the ZINATHA in Zimbabwe, the nganga of Tanzania, and the women of Thusano Lefatsheng in Botswana, not to mention other communities in Africa and the South. *This is piracy of herbs and blood samples from Africa.* This raises important moral issues. Don't these companies owe something to the people of Africa and the South for their knowledge and biodiversity? Also, what right do they have to then charge these people exorbitant prices for their drugs—or, alternatively, to let the people die rather than provide them with life-saving drugs?

But there are even larger moral issues than price. Piracy is one thing, but taking advantage of people's ignorance and vulnerability is another, and may be even more serious. The small farmers in the villages of Zimbabwe, Tanzania and Botswana did not even know that they had something of value that they were giving away for free. They did not know anything about 'intellectual property.' It reminds one of the lands stolen from Zimbabwe by the British in the 1890s, when the people did not even know that land could be 'privatised.' Later, King Lobengula of Matabeleland complained to Queen Victoria, only to be haughtily brushed aside. If the king was ignorant, that was his fault. Similarly, if the women of Thusano Lefatsheng in Botswana did not know about 'IP,' that was just 'too bad.'

This problem of ignorance is not unique to Africans. I was told on sound authority during my interview with the Chinese ambassador and his experts in Geneva that even the Chinese took time to understand the full implications of 'IP.' It is only in 1984, with the opening up of the Chinese economy, that China enacted a patent law that provided limited protection for 'IP' rights. However, it was not until 1992, during trade negotiations with the US, that China included patent protection for pharmaceutical products. But even then its implications were not fully clear. In 2002 China joined the WTO, and as part of fulfilling the conditions for joining, it had to accept compliance with TRIPS (Trade-Related Intellectual Property Rights). China was not party to the inclusion of TRIPS in the WTO. Nor for that matter was the rest of the South. As mentioned in the chapter on the WTO, TRIPS became 'trade-related' under pressure from the pharmaceutical industry.

During the 1970s and 1980s many countries in the South—such as India, Brazil, and Cuba—had encouraged manufacturing of local generics. It was this that the pharmaceutical conglomerates wanted to stifle, if not kill outright. That was the origin of TRIPS and the application of the WTO's enforcement mechanism on a matter which should never have been part of the WTO. Matters dealing with health should have remained with the WHO, and those dealing with biodiversity with the Convention on Biological Diversity.

The Doha Declaration on TRIPS and Public Health

The fight over TRIPS had been going on at the WTO for many years. Within the WTO the battle has to be fought using the peculiar WTO legalistic language. At a critical time, just before the WTO Doha Ministerial in 2001, the responsibility for shepherding the public health issue was passed on to Zimbabwe. I was then part of the team from my NGO base in Harare—SEATINI—and soon I was in contact with Ambassador Chidyausiku and his deputy Tadeous Chifamba in Geneva. I had met Ambassador Lt. Col. (Retd.) Boniface G. Chidyausiku first in China, where he was Zimbabwe's ambassador in the 1980s. He is a tough-minded relentless 'fighter'; he and Chifamba worked day and night—in conjunction with several ambassadors from the countries of the South—to negotiate an amendment to the TRIPS agreement. This, then, was the basis of the Doha Ministerial Declaration on TRIPS and Public Health. I was at Doha as a member of the Uganda delegation.

The adoption of this declaration was very significant, and so I provide some excerpts.[71]

Following a preamble that recognised 'the gravity of the public health problems' afflicting developing countries, the declaration set out the new rules and 'flexibilities' under TRIPS:

- The TRIPS agreement 'can and should be interpreted and implemented in a manner supportive of WTO members' right to protect public health and, in particular, to promote access to medicines for all.'
- The members recognised the 'flexibilities' to include: 'the right to grant compulsory licences and the freedom to determine the grounds upon which such licences are granted.'
- Each member had a right 'to determine what constitutes a national emergency . . . it being understood that public health crises, including those relating to HIV/AIDS, tuberculosis, malaria and other epidemics, can represent a national emergency.'
- On the issue of the TRIPS provision regarding the 'exhaustion of intellectual property rights,' each member was 'free to establish its own regime for such exhaustion without chal-

lenge, subject to the MFN and national treatment provisions of Articles 3 and 4.'

Although the TRIPS agreement was now amended, it took a long time for developing countries to apply the 'flexibilities' provided for in the Doha Declaration. In the wake of globalisation, the countries of the South have been obliged to open their doors to foreign direct investments, and the pharmaceutical sector was one of the first to be seized upon by the mega-drug companies of the West. And when they could not destroy the existing local companies in the South, the Western mega-pharmaceuticals took them and their governments to court for allegedly violating their patents— as the following example shows.

Novartis Cases against India and South Africa

Prior to signing TRIPS, Indian law allowed patents on the *process* of producing a drug, not on the *product* itself. The difference, in this particular case, is that *imatinib*, a product produced by Novartis and used in drugs to treat certain types of cancer, could not be patented; only the process of making it could. Novartis charged $ 2666 per patient per month for *imatinib*; Indian generic companies—like CIPLA—could produce and sell it for between $177 and $266 per patient per month. But because the law did not allow product patents, Novartis could not patent *imatinib*. However, as soon as India changed the law in 2005 to allow for product patents in order to conform to TRIPS, Novartis took India to court for violating TRIPS with regard to *imatinib*. It was waiting for this moment. The complaint was immediately contested by Indian generic drug companies and some NGO advocacy groups. It was a long trial. Finally, on 1 April 2013, the Indian Supreme Court ruled in favour of the latter. Novartis lost. What is extremely important is that the Intellectual Property Appellate Board—which hears appeals from the decisions of the Indian patent office—explicitly considered the public health implications of the high price charged for the drug by Novartis in India. The Board held that 'the drug . . . in our view is too unaffordable to poor cancer patients in India. Thus, we also observe that a grant of product patent on this application can create havoc in the lives of poor people and their families affected with the cancer for which this drug is effective. This will have disastrous effects on society as well.'[72]

This was a landmark case, for it answers some of the ethical issues I had raised earlier relating to the immorality of drug companies that put profits above the lives of people. These transnational corporations take advantage of the vulnerabilities of the countries of the South when they are faced with the implications of international agreements—such as TRIPS—that they were never party to during their negotiation, but which they are forced accept upon joining the WTO. Regarding the earlier narrative based on my experience in Africa, I would add that TRIPS and similar international agreements also raise the larger issues of knowledge production and its appropriation by global capitalist corporations. *They not only steal this knowledge from poor communities in Africa (and elsewhere in the South). They also turn around and take Southern governments to court for 'violating' the 'engineered and patented knowledge' these corporations produce using the pirated knowledge of the people of the South.*

What the Novartis case has also illustrated is that the governments of the South are now waking up to their responsibility to their people, often pushed by civil society, as in the case in India. South Africa had a similar experience. In 2012, taking advantage of South Africa's adherence to TRIPS, Novartis took the South African government to court for allowing the cheaper cancer drugs from CIPLA, the Indian generics company, on the market. Access to CIPLA's anti-retroviral medicines has been vital for providing life-prolonging treatment to more than 1.2 million patients. But the big drug monopolies have used TRIPS to block access to generic medicines in South Africa, especially since the end of apartheid in 1994. These monopolies are supported by Western governments that have used Bilateral Investment Treaties and Free Trade Agreements to impose strengthened TRIPS-Plus IPR protection, specifically on 'compulsory licensing' (see below) and data protection. Furthermore, unlike India, South Africa had granted several patents to Novartis for *imatinib*. In addition, whilst India had laws against 'evergreening,' by which drug companies like Novartis maintain artificially high prices on medicines by continually extending patent protection for 'minor modifications' to existing drugs, South African law had no such provision.

So the odds were against the South African government when Novartis took it to court in 2012. On 11 July 2012 a hundred NGO activists demonstrated before South Africa's parliament, pleading for the court to reject the Novartis case when it became known that the court might rule in favour of Novartis. There were similar demonstrations in Johannesburg and Cape Town by hundreds of activists, including activists from Medicins Sans Frontières. I will wind things down here and skip over the technical details to say that in this war between Novartis and the people, the people won.

THE STRUGGLE TO GET DEVELOPMENT ON WIPO'S AGENDA

The Doha Declaration on TRIPS and Public Health had shown us how the South, when united, could change certain elements embedded in the existing system of international governance crafted by the North. For a long time the South has been challenging the Northern monopoly on knowledge and innovation, but this is a long and difficult war. During the four years I was at the South Centre (2005–2009) the industrialised North had blocked the WIPO from putting development on its agenda. This might surprise some, for the North never stops paying lip service to the notion of development. It had already become a part of the agenda of the WTO when the word 'development' was added as the middle name of the Doha Round (Doha Development Round). So how could they block it in the WIPO?

The South Centre is not an NGO. As it is an intergovernmental organisation (IGO), my colleagues and I could enter WIPO, and thus get involved in direct interaction with negotiators. In the early months we found to our dismay that the South was not united. Often, developed countries used their divide-and-rule tactics to separate Africa, for example, from the rest of the South, or the LDCs from the DCs. Apart from a few countries such as India, Brazil and Cuba, very few of them really understood the IP system. Because of this lack of knowledge they were often distracted into addressing marginal rather than key issues, especially when the carrot of 'aid' was dangled before them.

The IP division at the South Centre was led by Xuan Li, mentored by Professor Carlos Correa (a well-known expert and author of several books on IP) and assisted, among others, by Viviana Munoz. Xuan used to organise late evening or early morning meetings with a number of delegations from the South to discuss the technical intricacies of TRIPS and the WIPO agreements. She was helped in this process by previous work done by a number of activist NGOs, such as the Third World Network, the Center for International Environmental Law, Genetic Resources Action International, Health Action International, and Quakers United Nations Office. Gradually, a solid 'third-world front' was built within the walls of the magnificent—transparent and yet opaque—glass edifice of WIPO. Brazil had a very active and informed delegation at WIPO. It initiated the creation of a group called 'Group of the Friends of Development,' which met often to plan the group's strategy and coordinate the work of the developing countries. Finally, on 28 September 2007 the General Assembly of WIPO passed a resolution incorporating 'development' as part of WIPO's mandate.

The Battle against the West's Backdoor Methods to Undermine the South's Effort to Industrialise

However, having lost the 'development' battle at WIPO, the West quickly shifted the theatre of war from WIPO to other less well-known agencies of 'global governance'—such as the World Customs Organisation, the Global Congress on Counterfeiting and Piracy, and the Standards Employed by Customs for Uniform Rights Enforcement (SECURE).

In January 2008, Xuan Li discovered that the Fourth Global Congress on Counterfeiting and Piracy was going to be held in Dubai in February. The South Centre was not invited. Xuan asked me, as the head of the Secretariat, what we should do. After some discussion, we decided that invitation or no invitation, the Centre had to be present at Dubai. Xuan and our press and internet expert, Vikas Nath, bought the airline tickets, packed an enormous bag full of South Centre publications and posters, and went to Dubai. Since they were not allowed in the conference center, they set up their own *'little ad hoc counter workshop'* in a hotel near the conference site. The objective was to make border and customs officers from the South aware that they were being used by the rich countries and their corporations to impose IP protection regimes on their behalf.

Under SECURE (a tantalising abbreviation), the OECD countries had hoped to empower customs officials to inspect, seize *and destroy* goods imported into the countries of the South that the corporations from the rich countries would identify as violating intellectual property rights. So, incredibly, the Western mega-corporations wanted customs officials in the South to act as their agents, to work for them as 'border guards' or watchdogs of IP enforcement, and to give them authority well beyond their existing mandate. The standards included in the provisional SECURE on 'IPR Legislative and Enforcement Regime Development' represented a significant departure from the prevailing standards of the TRIPS agreement. For example, according to TRIPS, border measures applied only to importation of counterfeit trademarks or pirated copyright goods. There is a significant distinction between IPR violations and product falsification (e.g., in pharmaceuticals). SECURE went far beyond the provisions of TRIPS. Furthermore, there were economic and legal aspects of enforcement costs that were not fully understood, let alone incorporated, in the calculations of customs administrations in the countries of the South. In other words, the developed countries were trying to promote a 'TRIPS-Plus-Plus' agenda on international border enforcement through the backdoor. Although the SECURE Standards were termed by the WCO as 'voluntary,' the danger was that in the future these (voluntary standards) could evolve into mandatory standards—as has often happened in the past with other such 'voluntary' initiatives.

In Dubai, the South Centre`s *'little ad hoc counter workshop'* displayed posters and literature to correct the false information provided by the OECD 'experts.' Xuan Li and Vikas Nath also learnt that the donors from the West were enticing the South's customs officers to attend 'capacity building' courses in the shining cities of the West—all flights paid for, plus per diems. In a matter of a day the SC's 'side event' became a major attraction for the customs officials of the South. They picked up the SC literature and talked with Xuan and Vikas; for the first time, they were exposed to a different perspective than the dominant WTO- WIPO perspective, especially on the very complex and technical subject of IP enforcement.

The South Centre supports the harmonisation of IP enforcement rules (I must repeat that I am opposed to the whole notion of privatisation of knowledge), but if enforcement measures are to be put in place, these should be done in harmony with the development agenda now adopted by the WIPO, and in conformity with the flexibilities as provided in the Doha Declaration on TRIPS and Public Health.

CONCLUSION

Property rights confer control over resources. The owners can then exploit these pretty much as they will. In the present capitalist system, the intellectual property regime has resulted in surrendering people's knowledge of the world's seeds and biodiversity (to name only two things), which are part of the 'global common,' to the will of mega corporations. The IP system is a relatively new development even within the evolution of capitalism. It violates all principles of natural justice, and it is dangerous for millions of poor people. It must be phased out.

The notion that without IP protection, innovation would be stifled is an ideological position created and propagated by those that benefit from the privatisation of knowledge. I came to a diametrically opposite conclusion over two decades of work with farming communities in Tanzania, Zimbabwe, Botswana, and much of eastern and southern Africa. Ordinary peasants and workers are amazingly innovative and productive, until their resources and knowledge are appropriated and corporatised, and the people enslaved to earn profits for corporations.

The institutions of global governance, including the WTO and the WIPO, are creations of an asymmetrical world dominated by the early industrialisers of the imperial North. They have no interest in helping the South to industrialise and compete against them in the exploitation of the world's diminishing natural resources. *Attempts by the countries of the South to challenge this system have provoked aggressive action by the industrialised West, in ways that can justly be described as acts of war.* They use the existing legal order that they created to criminalise those that fight against the unjust system. The examples from the seed and pharmaceutical industries provide ample evidence of this. The North tries to divide and rule the South. When the South, against all odds, manages to unite and fight back (as in the WTO and the WIPO), the West counter-attacks using its money and market power, directly or through institutions such as the World Customs Organisation, the Global Congress on Counterfeiting and Piracy, SECURE and several other Western-dominated organisations.

International regulatory regimes, such as the Kyoto Protocol and the Biodiversity Protocol, are too weak against the big and powerful players like the US and the EU and their mega-corporations. This is not an argument for not trying to change the trade regime through the WTO—for although the WTO is unreformable, it is politically imperative that it must be constantly challenged—or the IP regime through WIPO, or the climate regime through the United Nations Framework Convention for Climate Change. This is a cautionary note against putting too much faith in these institutions. Developing countries must have faith in themselves. They must harness their own innovative capacity and build alternative models of development, whilst always trying to abide by their international obligations as interpreted in a fair manner, and working towards a just and humane global society.

5. TRADE SANCTIONS AS ACTS OF WAR

Trade and sanctions go together. Sanctions are acts of war. They fall just short of and often precede actual military action.

INTRODUCTION

I have chosen four countries as illustrative examples. One is Uganda, where I come from. The second is Zimbabwe—I have lived there for twenty-three years. Third and fourth are Cuba and Iran—where my familiarity is less, but I have travelled in these two countries under sanctions several times during my tenure as the Executive Director of the South Centre. Cuba has been under US sanctions since July 1960, Iran since 1979, and Zimbabwe since 2002. Uganda was one of the earliest countries to have gone through a 'regime change' engineered by its former colonial power, Britain. This gives me a long-enough time span—more than five decades—to look at them in hindsight. Hopefully this will provide some insights into the regime of sanctions as part of trade war.

I have been arguing all along that the developed countries are not interested in the development of the rest of the world. In chapter two I showed that the WTO is an extended arm of US/EU trade policy. The US and the EU talk a lot about the 'free market,' but in practice they are as protectionist as the rest of the world—if not even more so. I gave the example of the four West

African countries ('the Cotton Four') where the lives and livelihoods of millions are put at stake by US subsidies and protectionist policies. Profit, not human rights, is what essentially motivates the developed capitalist world. In chapter three, I analysed this phenomenon—profits before people—in relation to the Euro-African Economic Partnership Agreement (EPA), which is essentially an agency to service the interests of European corporations. This asymmetrical relationship has been built over a century. It has created institutions and structures that are embedded in the culture and behaviour of both sides of the divide. In chapter four I traced the dominance of the West's technological superiority over the Rest—a relatively new development (barely three hundred years old) which continues to exploit (through, for example, bio-piracy) and appropriate the traditional knowledge systems of the South. All this 'stolen' knowledge—knowledge that should never have been privatised—is encased in a flawed and unjust system called 'intellectual property.'

STATUS QUO VERSUS REVISIONIST NATIONS

Every civilisation, ours included, has a set of institutions responsible for producing a certain kind of order—moral as well as physical—and a set of ideas that define, elaborate and justify that order and how changes can 'legitimately' take place within it. 'Legitimacy' is defined by those who wield power in the international system. We call these 'mainstream' or dominant ideas. In our time, these ideas are the products of the institutional thinking of the World Bank, the IMF, the WTO, the OECD 'think tanks,' and the universities and research institutions which reflect on these matters and produce a certain kind of knowledge. Mainstream ideas on any matter of consequence in contemporary times—whether it is economics, human rights, governance, trade and investment, development, or causes of conflict and approaches to peace—are the products of these institutions.[73] These are the powers and institutions of 'order' or, if you like, the 'status quo.' This does not mean they are opposed to change, but they are opposed to a fundamental alteration of the system—the system of capitalist production and exchange.

Then there are those who would want to change the system fundamentally. They reject the prevailing system in favour of some other system of production and exchange—for example, a 'socialist' or 'Islamic' order. They are the 'revolutionaries.' Yet, not all those who reject the present order are revolutionaries. Many may challenge certain aspects of the present order, whilst not rejecting its fundamental foundational principles. Certain Islamic tendencies are not necessarily against the capitalist order, but they have their own views about production, distribution, social justice, and governance. I call them, collectively, 'revisionists'—they seek to reorder the system in some fundamental or significant ways.

All this might sound rather abstract—or, probably, too simplified a version of something that is very complex. Whatever one's view, it is necessary to understand these terms. 'Capitalist,' 'socialist,' 'Islamic,' 'order,' 'status quo,' 'revolutionaries,' 'revisionist' and other terms are fairly common—not only in academic literature but also in the media and even in popular conversation. So, for example, America is 'capitalist' and in favour of the 'status quo,' or Cuba is 'socialist' and 'revolutionary.' We need these concepts when we pose questions, such as: Why has the United States imposed sanctions against Iran or Cuba? Why have the Western countries ganged up against Zimbabwe? What kind of 'order' is it that Cuba, Iran and Zimbabwe appear to be threatening? It is impossible to escape these concepts and these questions. The very notion of sanctions in international relations raises strong political, legal, and moral issues that often generate deep passions, even violence. Sanctions, after all, are, as I argue, acts of war.

There are thus competing ideas about contemporary order and its moral basis coming out of 'radical intellectuals' from Latin America, Asia, and Africa. These are in many ways fundamentally different from those of the 'mainstream' thinking. And even if the West and the Rest share some common values—human rights and democracy, for example—their application in concrete situations can raise serious problems. That is why countries—like Cuba, Iran and Zimbabwe—that espouse 'alternative' conceptions of order (on the issue of land and property, for example) are regarded as 'out of order.' They are then 'legitimate' targets for sanctions by the dominant power(s), with the aim of bringing them 'back to order.'

TRADE SANCTIONS: LEARNING FROM SOME CASE STUDIES
The Political Economy of Sanctions

One of the abiding features of our time is that the imperial countries—through colonisation and through their corporations—have established control over the resources of the colonised people. If there is any attempt by the colonised people to exercise control of these resources, then the imperial countries come with hammer and tongs to restore their imperial control. This invariably involves sanctions, but might also lead to 'regime change.'[74]

Uganda

I learnt the above lesson first hand. I was born and grew up in Uganda. As I matured I realised that Asian immigrants—including industrialists like Madhvani and Mehta and my own family—were essentially servicing British colonial and commercial interests. Britain directly or indirectly, controlled practically all the resources of the country.

Uganda became 'independent' in October 1962. In October 1969 the parliament endorsed President Obote's *'Common Man's Charter'* as a set of 'First Steps for Uganda to Move to the Left.' In his speech, Obote made a commitment to democracy and insisted that the country's resources were needed to develop the people of Uganda. He said that the fruits of development would be shared fairly and equitably amongst the people. Then he took what turned out to be a bold and risky step. In May 1970, he nationalised eighty-five private enterprises, including the three British banks—Barclays, National and Grindlays, and Standard Bank—that directly or indirectly controlled some 80 percent of commercial assets in Uganda. He promised to compensate the banks. But this was not enough. The whole 'move to the Left' was anathema to the former colonial power. The move set off a chain reaction—domestic and international—which ended on 25 January 1971 with Obote's removal from power by a military coup engineered by Britain and Israel—a fact whose evidence is now available in public documents.

That was my first experience of neocolonial imperialism. I was then still a young radical nationalist . . . and naive. I had helped Obote draft the 'Common Man's Charter,' and had imagined that political independence opened the doors to economic independence. It is possible that Obote, though a very astute and mature nationalist, had thought the same. We were both wrong. Britain and Israel took advantage of ethnic and historical divisions among the people and leadership of Uganda, carried out a 'regime change' using Uganda's army, and restored British control over Uganda's resources and economy. As for me and my family, we were forced out of Uganda by the military regime of Idi Amin. I joined the democratic struggle against Amin's brutal regime. In 1979, eight years after Amin's installation into power, he was ousted by the combined action of Tanzanian and Uganda guerrilla forces. I went back to Uganda, now as member of the Uganda National Liberation Front (UNLF). In May 1980, there was yet another military coup that ousted the UNLF government. I was forced into my second political exile.

I will not go further into this story. The point is made. Uganda is a small country, physically almost the same size as England. But England controlled the destiny of Uganda—of course not without resistance from the people of Uganda. But it is a struggle. After the Second World War, British imperialism was replaced by the collective imperialism of Europe over Africa. In an earlier chapter I narrated how Europe had used the threat of trade sanctions to force on the East African Community an unequal treaty—the Economic Partnership Agreement—that would seriously damage East Africa's prospect for industrialisation. But now, fast forwarding to our time, the rise of BRICS gives Africa options to attempt to decouple from the US and Europe.[75]

Zimbabwe

In 1980 Zimbabwe had just won 'independence' after more than a decade of guerrilla war. I was then in my second political exile in Kenya. After 1980 I shifted my exile to Zimbabwe, which became my second home. What struck me immediately was the difference between Uganda and Zimbabwe. It was principally the land issue that defined this difference. At the Lancaster House 'independence' negotiations, Mugabe had made two vital concessions: one, he would allow the white minority a number of reserved seats in the new parliament; and two, he would not touch the land for ten years, and let it be exchanged on a 'willing seller, willing buyer' basis. Shridath Ramphal, then the Secretary-General of the Commonwealth, had mediated the agreement on this contentious issue. At a critical moment of the talks, he had phoned the US ambassador in London and through him received a commitment from President Carter that the US would contribute 'substantial funds' to secure land distribution to the people of Zimbabwe and that he would secure similar guarantees from the British.[76]

After Zimbabwe's independence, land prices shot up. The 'willing seller, willing buyer' agreement became practically useless for Africans who wanted land. Few white owners were prepared to sell land at a time when the prices were rising. The very people who had obstructed Zimbabwe's independence became, ironically, its beneficiaries soon after independence.

During those years I worked closely with the General Agricultural and Plantation Workers Union and the Zimbabwe Congress of Trade Unions. I travelled extensively in rural areas. I had seen the dire effects of the government's failure to undertake much-needed land reform. President Mugabe had scrupulously maintained the terms of the Lancaster agreement. Several efforts were made to resolve the financial and technical issues with the British government. At one time, I was hired as a consultant by the United Nations Development Programme (UNDP) in Harare to look into the land issue. Following my research, I advised the UNDP that a proper audit of the land be carried out, and if there was goodwill between the Zimbabwean and British governments, the land issue could be resolved peacefully within five years.

I am convinced that with patient diplomacy, the land issue could have been resolved. The British Prime Minister John Major nearly did resolve the issue in consultation with the Zimbabwean government. But soon afterwards, Major lost the elections, and Tony Blair took over power, with Clare Short as the Secretary of State for International Development (1997–2003). Blair simply reneged on all Lancaster House agreements—promises that even

Margaret Thatcher was careful not to disown. Up to this day, few people in the West know this side of the story.

Under pressure from the War Veterans Association, Mugabe fast-tracked the land reform in 2000. Paradoxically, Blair, who was at the heart of creating the land crisis in Zimbabwe, imposed sanctions on Zimbabwe. He persuaded the NATO countries and the European Union to impose a series of 'targeted sanctions' against Zimbabwe. In 2013, former President Mbeki of South Africa claimed in an interview with Al-Jazeera that Blair had put pressure on him to help Britain overthrow Mugabe militarily.[77]

To this day, Zimbabwe has been under Western sanctions. A holdover from colonial times, the land issue could have been resolved. But it has become a festering sore on the body politic of Zimbabwe, and in relations between Zimbabwe and the West. Efforts by the West to encourage 'regime change' through vilifying Mugabe and through financing opposition parties have failed to dislodge Mugabe. I was involved in the 1990s democratic movement to create a multi-party system in Zimbabwe. But the moment that funds began to pour in from Europe and America to support the opposition, I left the movement. Outside funding delegitimised the democratic process—as indeed, it would if Africa or China were to finance opposition parties in Europe or America. Arguments by the West claiming that Zimbabwe suffers from a 'democracy deficit' are hypocritical. They unjustifiably exonerate the West from its share of responsibility in the continuing crisis in relations between Zimbabwe and the West.

This too, like Uganda, is a long story. But the point is made. Zimbabwe, like Uganda, is a neocolonial state. The people want land and control of their resources to enjoy the economic fruits of political independence. But this has been denied to the people by an imperialist order.

For centuries Cuba was a part of the Spanish Empire. In the late nineteenth century, Cuban revolutionaries rebelled against Spain. In the wake of the Spanish-American War (1898), the US invaded the island, and in 1902 installed a government to rule the new Republic of Cuba. Cuba in effect became a neo-colony of the United States.

On 1 January 1959, after nearly six years of guerrilla war led by Fidel Castro and Che Guevara, the Cuban revolutionaries overthrew the US-supported Batista regime and declared Cuba a socialist state. This was followed by a program of nationalisation and major social reforms, including access to medical facilities, health, housing, communications, education, and equal rights for women. Beyond Cuba, Castro started a vigorous programme of solidarity and support for liberation struggles in other parts of the Global South, including Algeria, Angola, Nicaragua and Yemen, among others.

Fearing that Communist insurgencies would spread throughout the nations of the South, the United States made a number of unsuccessful attempts to overthrow the Cuban government, including the abortive Bay of Pigs Invasion of 1961. This was followed soon afterwards with the Cuban Missile Crisis in 1962.[78] In return for Soviet withdrawal of missiles from Cuba, the United States promised not to invade Cuba in the future.

Even before Bay of Pigs and the missile crisis, the US had imposed sanctions on Cuba. They began on 19 October 1960, and covered a whole range of products, processes and procedures. They continue to this day and are some of the most far-reaching sanctions in scope. For example, the 'Cuban Assets Control Regulations,' enforced by the US Treasury Department, affect all American citizens and permanent residents wherever they are located, all people and organisations physically located in the United States, and all branches and subsidiaries of US organisations throughout the world.[79] One of these regulations—the 1992 'Cuban Democracy Act'—is quite interesting. It stipulates that all diplomatic and commercial sanctions should be maintained as long as Cuba refuses to move toward 'democratisation and greater respect for human rights.' One has to come from one of the neo-colonies of the West in order to appreciate the hypocrisy of this act. Human rights organisations, such as the Inter-American Commission on Human Rights, Amnesty International, and Human Rights Watch, have been arguing that US sanctions on Cuba have no legal or moral basis in international law.

To make an assessment of the causes and effects of this six-ty-year-old sanctions apparatus is extremely complicated. It is like trying to shoot at a moving target. 2014 is not the same as 1960. The world is not the same. Above all, Cuban-American relations are symbolic of the David-Goliath battle; little Cuba, barely a hundred kilometres from American shores, is holding on its own (with solidarity support from outside, including progressive forces within the United States). Cuba is also probably the only 'Communist' state in the world with the same political party and movement (for it is more than just a political party) in power as when the sanctions began. Fidel Castro yielded to his brother Raúl in 2008, and though there are differences in posture and style, Raúl (in my view) is only a contemporary version of Fidel, given the dramatic changes in the world and in the trans-American political economy in the last sixty years.

Within the American subcontinent, a new wind is blowing. It is the Bolivarian wind. The *Movimiento Continental Bolivariano* (Bolivarian Continental Movement), named after the famous historical and emblematic figure Simón Bolívar, was founded in Venezuela on 8 December 2009 by a group of 950 left-wing activists from twenty-six Latin American nations, committed to fighting against imperialism and promoting the interests of workers in the continent. This is new. For too long (nearly five hundred years) Latin American countries have been under the heel of first the European imperial powers and then Pax Americana. The figure that inspired the movement—Hugo Chávez– is dead, but he has left his legacy—*Chavismo*—behind to guide his less boisterous successor, Nicolás Maduro.

The Bolivarian revolution and Chavismo are important because you cannot understand the present situation in Cuba under enduring US sanctions without putting these within the larger context of the evolving politics of the region. During the Cold War, the Soviet Union held Castro's hand. The collapse of the Soviet Union in 1989 left Cuba almost on its own to fend off American sanctions. The US thought it had finally caught Castro and Cuba in its cage. For sure, it was the most difficult time for Cuba, labelled by the people of Cuba as the 'Special Period' when Castro had to oblige his people through the severest test to withstand American sanctions. Castro even compromised on the economy and opened the doors to tourism and some foreign investments.

With the rise of Hugo Chávez (who regarded Fidel as his 'father'), the fate of Cuba changed. Venezuela supplied Cuba with an estimated 110,000 barrels of oil a day in exchange for the services of some 44,000 Cubans, mostly doctors and nurses. In July 2014, Russian President Vladimir Putin toured six countries in Latin America. He met with President Castro and cancelled 90 percent of Cuba's $32 billion debt to Russia, ending a two-decade argument. Of course, the hidden context is the war in Ukraine, where the US is deeply involved in an anti-Russian campaign. So Putin said to the US, If you play in my backyard, I play in yours.

So if Raúl Castro appears to be a milder version of his elder brother, that is because Raúl can afford to smile a little. The situation is not as desperate as during the 'Special Period.'

In the meantime, Barack Obama's ascendance to the presidency had initially raised hopes that he might lift or reduce the sanctions. But these hopes were quickly dashed. Obama made the lifting of sanctions subject to Cuba improving on human rights and freedoms. Some American business leaders have been advocating the lifting of the sanctions, arguing that it would be good for American business. Gary Hart, former US Senator, added his voice by openly saying that the sanctions were 'irrational' and a product of the influence of first-generation Cuban-Americans.[80] George Shultz, who served as Secretary of State under Reagan, has described the continued embargo as 'insane.'

In 2006, the US government created a task force to monitor the implementation of the sanctions even more vigorously. Criminal penalties for violating the embargo included up to ten years in prison, $1 million in corporate fines, $250,000 in individual fines, and civil penalties reached as high as $55,000 per violation. In over fifty years of sanctions, the United States has been almost completely isolated in the United Nations. Since 1992, every year, the General Assembly has passed a resolution saying that the US sanctions constitute a violation of the UN charter.

Despite this diplomatic isolation of the US, the sanctions remain in place.[81] But the world knows that little Cuba has beaten the American Goliath. The American ambition to cage Cuba after the collapse of the USSR has been defeated. This is indeed quite remarkable. Cuba and Castro continue to remain a beacon of hope for the countries and peoples of the South. If little Cuba can do it, why not the much larger Iran?

Iran

Iran, like Cuba, is another case of defiance against US-spearheaded sanctions, probably the second longest case of sanctions after Cuba. Sanctions against Iran began in 1979—some thirty years ago. Children born in Iran that year have lived under US and European sanctions all their lives. Now they are mature young men and women who for thirty years have gone through the ups and downs of the Iranian Revolution.

Like in the case of Cuba, it is the United States that has initiated and pushed for sanctions while Europe, generally, has been a reluctant participant. Like in Cuba, the sanctions are quite comprehensive. But there are important differences. In Cuba the nuclear issue came to a near blow-up, but it was diffused within a relatively short time. In Iran it is the centre of the deadlock between the US and Iran. Iran claims it wants the nuclear energy to supplement its depleting oil resources. The US and Israel (especially Israel) claim that Iran wants nuclear power to wage war. They claim that Iranian nuclear potential is a threat to 'global peace and security.' And so, the sanctions cannot be lifted until the nuclear issue is first resolved to the satisfaction of US, Israel, and Europe.

Hence, Iran is under an array of sanctions mounted by the NATO countries. These include:

- A total economic and financial embargo;
- Sanctions on the energy sector, which provides about 80 percent of government revenues;
- Sanctions on the sale of aircraft or repair parts to Iranian aviation companies;
- Sanctions on Iranians engaging in any transactions with American citizens;

- An information embargo, including on the state broadcasting authority. The US and the West do not want the rest of the world to hear the Iranian side of the story;
- Sanctions on major Iranian electronics producers;
- Sanctions on internet policing agencies such as the Iranian Cyber Police;
- The Communications Regulatory Authority;
- In addition, the US has imposed sanctions on companies doing business with Iran. A license from the Treasury Department is required to do business with Iran. Any United States property held by blacklisted companies and individuals are subject to confiscation.[82]

The US is supported by the NATO 'coalition of the willing' states:

- Israel has declared Iran an enemy state. It penalises foreign companies that trade with Iran, and has put in place elaborate mechanisms to implement sanctions;
- The EU has quite comprehensive sanctions measures covering trade and financial and other services (e.g., shipping);
- Canada has put a ban on Iranian national property deals, a ban on arms and oil technology, as well as a ban on investments in Iran;
- Australia has imposed financial sanctions and a travel ban on individuals and entities involved in Iran's nuclear and missile programs;
- Switzerland has banned trade with Iran in dual-purpose arms and products used in oil and gas sectors, and a ban on financial services;
- Japan has banned some Iranian banks and investments in Iran's energy sector, and has frozen the assets of some individuals

(but interestingly, Japan has not imposed a trade ban on oil, for Japan needs Iran's oil);

- South Korea has imposed targeted sanctions on 126 Iranian individuals and companies.

There is a difference between Cuba and Iran. Iran is a big country strategically located in the center of a war zone. However, like Cuba, which offers an alternative development programme (a socialist vision), Iran offers an alternative programme based on the Shia interpretation of Sharia. So both Cuba and Iran, in terms of my vocabulary, are 'revisionist' states; they do not accept the 'imperial peace' and their conceptions of democracy and good governance are not the same as that of the US and the West.

Like in the case of Cuba, it is difficult to assess the impact of Western sanctions on Iran. There is no question that it hurts Iran's economy. The chairman of the Majlis Planning and Budget Committee said that the West has frozen an equivalent of $100 billion of Iran's money in foreign banks since the 1979 Iranian Revolution. But the damage is not all one-sided. The trade and financial sanctions have left a big hole in Iran-Western relations, but that hole is substantially filled by the BRICS countries. BRICS do not share Western enthusiasm for sanctions against Iran. Oil is a major resource. Iran is able to barter oil for goods and services from the BRICS countries. India, for example, pays for some Iranian oil imports in rupees. This is potentially damaging to the supremacy of the 'mighty' US dollar.

Also, Iran has cleverly used sanctions as a means to restructure its oil deals with foreign companies. Iran has set up a system of '*buyback contracts.*' The National Iranian Oil Company (NIOC) makes an agreement with a foreign corporation to jointly explore and develop an oil field. The foreign company deploys its technological services while NIOC remains in full control of the project. When the contract expires—usually after five to eight years—the Iranian state becomes the sole operator, keeping all revenues from further sales. And if a dispute arises between NIOC and the oil company, the matter might be taken out of the hands of the disputants by an Islamic court.[83]

This is in sharp contrast to the system forced on Iraq by the US. Under *'production-sharing agreements'* (PSA), the Iraqi state technically owns the oil, but its control is nominal. The PSA is just another name for the classic colonial form of concessions. It gives the foreign company monopoly rights to develop and manage an oil field for between twenty-five and forty years. During this period the terms of the contract are fixed and cannot be legally altered by the state. The reserves are entered into the company's balance sheets as the assets of the company, which is entitled to decide on the rates of their extraction (that is, their depletion) and other production details as it sees fit. There is no upper limit on profits. If disputes between the two arise, these are solved not in the courts of the host country, but in international arbitration tribunals where the company and the state are regarded as commercial partners with equal claims.[84]

The West thinks that sanctions-induced economic austerity will give rise to disaffection on the part of ordinary people, and thus 'eventually' to a regime change. This is an illusion the West has been harboring for thirty years. In thirty years, the West has learnt nothing of the deeply rooted anti-imperialist sentiment of the Iranian people.

CONCLUSION
The following chart is a simplified presentation of what is in fact a complex interplay of domestic and international forces. Trade,

THE GEOPOLITICS OF TRADE SANCTIONS

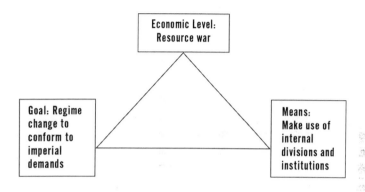

narrowly defined, is only a part of a wider nexus of imperial relations between the West and the Rest.

The four case studies I selected are each in their own way *sui generis*. But there are significant points of convergence between their various experiences. Regime change is common to all. The Empire managed to carry out a regime change in Uganda in 1971, but failed in Zimbabwe, Cuba and Iran—though not for lack of trying. In Cuba the US failed despite the CIA-sponsored Bay of Pigs invasion in April 1961. It would be interesting to try to understand why attempts by the Empire to bring about regime change succeeded in some cases (such as Libya in 2011) and failed in others (North Korea, for example). Would Gaddafi have survived if he had nuclear weapons? Is Iran safe because it refuses to abandon its nuclear energy program?

One of the reasons behind the success or failure of sanctions is the solidity of the sanctioned state. In Uganda, the Empire took advantage of internal ethnic divisions to oust Obote. In Zimbabwe, Cuba and Iran, there are divisions too, but the three states have proven to be resilient. Is that the reason, then, that the West accuses these regimes of suffering from a 'democracy deficit'? Is 'good governance' the Empire's war gambit to split these countries' soft underbellies in order to prepare the ground for regime change?

Finally, without being reductionist, it would be correct to say that the war for access to resources is a key to understanding the West's strategy in the South. In the chapter on EPAs, I cited the authority of the historian Robert Skidelsky to show how the US and Britain were vying for African resources in the period after the Second World War. I also showed how Europe is twisting the arm of African states to sign EPAs in order to have access to Africa's commodity resources for European industries. The resource war is part of the trade war.

Today, five billion people, arguably all in the South, starve so that a billion may live in comfort. It is odd that mainstream economists quote figures of 'growth' and prosperity even as the system of capitalism-imperialism is facing what looks like an epochal crisis. This is yet another example of the state of denial under which the West continues to pursue its relentless imperial hostilities all over the world. Could it be that the West needs wars to boost its arms industry in order to generate the 'growth' their economists talk about? What is known as military Keynesianism has its theorists—including, somewhat surprisingly, the Nobel Laureate Paul Krugman.[85] According to Neo-Keynesians, the United States was pulled out of the Great Depression of the 1930s by, among others events, the Second World War, and then following that, the Korean War (1950–53). They argue that wartime production increased aggregate demand, thus restoring the nation to prosperity.

It is no wonder, then, that there are 'revisionist nations'—which includes, broadly, the whole of the Global South—that want to change the world. This raises bigger issues of the strategy and tactics of transformation, to which I shall turn in the concluding chapter.

6. FROM WAR TO PEACE: THE THEORY AND PRACTICE OF REVOLUTIONARY CHANGE

'*Si vis pacem, para bellum*' is a Latin axiom translated as 'If you want peace, prepare for war.' In mainstream, realpolitik literature on international relations, mostly Anglo-Saxon, this is interpreted as meaning peace through overpowering military strength.[86] In the long run, this is a self-defeating adage. Whether the US has achieved peace in Iraq or Afghanistan or Iran through its overwhelming military power is an open question, but most people would say that it has not. Israel is a powerful state, but only in the military sense.

Appearances notwithstanding, the strong and powerful do not have it all their way. There is active resistance from below. People everywhere are innovating and finding new ways of fighting aggression, injustice and inequality, and alternative ways of organising production and exchange. A new world is taking shape, painfully but hopefully also peacefully.

ROOT CAUSES OF TRADE WARS

When looking for 'causes' of something disagreeable or unpleasant, there is a natural human temptation to blame somebody for it. However, it is important to clarify that when I analyzed the WTO or the WIPO or EPAs, I was not indulging in a 'blame game.' In international relations, it is important to understand

the difference between the popular or media tendency to blame someone, and trying to understand why individuals or nations or institutions do what they do. Understanding is not the same as blaming.

Blaming or finger-pointing is accusative; understanding is inquisitive. My approach to analysis is *inquisitive*—why do certain things happen?—not *accusative*.

There is another possible misunderstanding that I need to clarify before I proceed. I have used terms such as 'double standards' or 'hypocrisy' in describing the inconsistency between what Western countries claim (free trade, for example) and what they do in practice (protection). Again, these are not accusative terms. There is an ontological, verifiable reality behind such discrepancies between principles and actions. The West may claim (probably sincerely) that it is helping to 'develop' the south, while in reality it is impoverishing it. There is a whole school of political economy which argues that while the West claims to 'develop' the South, what they actually do is to 'underdevelop' it.[87]

It is important to understand three realities of trade war:

One: Imperialism;

Two: Resource wars; and

Three: Global Anarchy—the absence of a proper global governance structure.

DEFINING AND RECOGNISING THE REALITY OF IMPERIALISM

We must first come to terms with the concept—and reality—of imperialism. If one has not understood imperialism, one has understood nothing about the relationship between the North and the South, or between the West and the Rest.

Western Denial of the Reality of Imperialism

Paradoxically, people in the West, including well-meaning NGOs and people otherwise sympathetic to Africa, have difficulty recognising the reality of imperialism. Many people are in a state of denial about imperialism. I have sought to find an explanation in both Western culture and history to illuminate this mental blockage, but I have not come up with a good answer. For example, I have often wondered why Hitler is described in almost all Western literature as a 'fascist' but never as an imperialist. Could it be that calling Hitler an imperialist is too perilously close to looking at a mirror image? Today, many Westerners, including intellectuals, deny the existence of imperialism.

Since this is a rather important issue for this chapter, indeed for this book, I want to give a couple of examples from my experience. In November 1995, in Maastricht in the Netherlands, I was engaged in a public debate with Herman Cohen, a former US Under-Secretary of State for African Affairs, and at the time the governing executive of the Global Coalition for Africa (GCA).[88] The debate was on 'democracy and governance' in Africa. When I used the word 'imperialism' to describe the situation in Africa, Cohen countered by saying I was 'anachronistic,' and that imperialism was simply 'a figment of Tandon's imagination.' I did not have to answer him; Africans amongst the audience gave him several concrete examples of imperialism. One of these people was Aminata Traore, one-time Minister of Culture and Tourism in Mali. She told Cohen that she was disappointed that as a top official of the Global Coalition for Africa he had no understanding of imperialism or the reality of Africa.

In another instance, in February 1997 I attended a conference in Oslo on Agenda 21—i.e., sustainable development. I shared the platform with the influential consultant to the Brundtland Commission[89], Lloyd Timberlake. He was at the time also the Director of the World Business Council for Sustainable Development. He authored an empirically sound book on the state of the African environment. He countered my description of the present reality in Africa as dominated by imperialism by suggesting that I was 'out of date,' and that he had not heard the word imperialism 'for the last thirty years.' At first I was astonished, but then I realised that the audience—largely Norwegian—was probably in agreement with him. I had to tread carefully in order not to alienate my friends in the audience. So, without challenging Timberlake directly, I suggested—using an idiom I borrowed from my environmentalist friends—that because England can use Uganda's resources, its 'ecological footprint' is much bigger than Uganda's. I doubt if he understood my point, for he stared at me vacantly. He did not understand that this was because whilst Uganda had become 'independent,' England, as an imperial country, continued to exploit and consume Uganda's resources, and so had a bigger 'footprint.' I wondered, How does one 'educate' a person who is in a state of denial about the global political environment? Why should Timberlake's ecological environment be so real to him but not the political imperial environment? How did he manage to separate the two? I looked around expecting no support from the Norwegian audience. There was one exception, however—a young lady, Helene Bank. She told me during a coffee break that she agreed with me. She was later to join me to create SEATINI.

Imperialism Defined

Imperialism is a particular kind of relationship that arose in the wake of colonialism. It may not be reduced to just any kind of asymmetrical power relationship. Could the relations between the USA and Europe, for example, be described also as imperialist? No. Why not? Because although they have unequal power, at the global level they are *both* imperialist powers; they are *partners and competitors* at the same time. For instance, American and European companies compete in the telecommunications market. But if Zimbabwe, or Iran, or Cuba (or Syria, Somalia, or Venezuela) 'step out of line,' the US and the European Union will gang up to bring 'order'—cut off their gas and water, as it were, to 'bring them back into line.' No, imperialism is not *any* relationship between two unequal powers. It is a historically created phenomenon; you cannot discuss it in the abstract. Concretely, the imperialist nations compete and collaborate to maintain a system of production and consumption based on the exploitation of the rich resources—including labour—of the South.

Lenin's definition of imperialism as the 'highest stage of capitalism' is a good analytical extension of the Marxist theory of capital up to 1880s and beyond.[90] Students of international relations, especially those from the South, might want to read Lenin's classic on imperialism. Below I lay out imperialism's main characteristics as defined by Lenin:

1. Concentration of production and monopolies
2. The new role of banks
3. The emergence of finance capital and the financial oligarchy
4. Export of capital
5. Division of the world among capitalist associations
6. Division of the world among the great powers
7. Imperialism as a special stage of capitalism
8. Parasitism and decay of capitalism

Some mainstream Marxist writers still apply Lenin's basic analysis to the contemporary situation.[91] As may be seen, it is not a fleeting phenomenon; it is part of our present reality.

Fifty years after Lenin's book, Kwame Nkrumah, the first President of Ghana, wrote a book (whilst still President) entitled *Neo-Colonialism: The Last Stage of Imperialism.* This is what he wrote in the introduction: 'The neo-colonialism of today represents imperialism in its final and perhaps its most dangerous stage . . . . The essence of neo-colonialism is that the State which is subject to it is, in theory, independent and has all the outward trappings of international sovereignty. In reality, its economic system and thus its political policy is directed from outside.'[92]

Fifty years since Nkrumah's book, neo-colonialism—as defined by Nkrumah—is still with us. If anything, imperialism has become even more aggressive. Why? Because it is now under serious challenge from younger generations of third-world peoples and social activists, even in the West.

Are the BRICS Imperialist Countries?
There is a view that imperialism is not simply a Western phenomenon, that BRICS countries—Brazil, Russia, India, China and South Africa—are also imperialist or at least sub-imperialist.[93] *Are*

they not exploiting the cheap labour and resources of Africa?, they ask. *Are they not driving African manufacturers off the market with their cheap imports into Africa?* I have asked myself these questions many times.[94] My answer to this is related to the above description of imperialism as a historical phenomenon created during the rise of capitalism and its byproduct, colonialism.[95]

China and India traded with Africa for a thousand years but never colonised Africa.[96] What might happen in the future I do not know. Now they are both capitalist nations and might develop new forms of imperialist relations with Africa. There are undoubtedly asymmetrical power relations between China and African countries, just as there are asymmetrical power relations between the US and Europe. But in terms of their relationship, the US does not have imperial relations with, for example, the United Kingdom. In the same vein, Chinese relations with Africa are not imperial, nor sub-imperial.

Drawing from my experience in many agencies of global governance—such as the United Nations, the WTO, the WIPO, and others—there is much evidence of China and India (and Russia too) acting on the basis of 'solidarity' with African nations. In their own ways, China, India and Russia are also 'revisionist' states (as described in an earlier chapter); they too, like Africa, want to change the global order. In that sense they are on the same side of the divide between the West and the Rest. And no amount of distraction—mostly from the far left and the far right—can obscure the strategic question of building alliances and solidarities between BRICS and African and other third-world nations.

RESOURCE WARS

The second significant aspect of contemporary reality is resource wars. I give brief accounts of two such instances from Africa.

Nigeria

In Nigeria, the smuggling of refined oil products across porous West African borders has been going on for decades.[97] This parallel flow enables communities dependent on oil to organise their perilous lives and livelihoods outside of the formal sector. At the same time, multinational oil corporations (with Shell in the lead) have been selling under-invoiced oil in the global market for decades. They carry the Nigerian state in tow, with the ruling elite sharing the profits of this officially sanctioned under-priced oil.[98] In 1995, Ken Saro-Wiwa—writer, television producer, winner of the Right Livelihood Award, and president of the Movement for the Survival of the Ogoni People—was hanged by the military regime. His crime was to wage a nonviolent struggle against the environmental degradation of the land and waters of Ogoniland by an oil industry that benefits global corporations plus a couple of thousand Nigerian elites at the cost of millions.

This encapsulates the complex saga of the 'oil war' in Africa. In 2013, Al Jazeera released a four-part documentary series—*The Secret of Seven Sisters*—that showed how Western corporations dominate oil cartels and make secret pacts to control the world's oil.

Somalia

Somalia is an even more complex situation than Nigeria. I give a longer account of this because it is so little understood.

The dominant narrative vilifying Somalia as a 'failed state' is not persuasive; it leaves room to ask some legitimate questions that are not answered in this narrative. Somalia is disparaged the world over for hosting Al Shabaab and the pirates who have terrorised maritime fishing for several years. A significant and legitimate question to ask is: Does Somali piracy have anything to do with illegal fishing by European, American and Japanese fleets? Or with the illegal dumping of toxic (including nuclear) waste, devastating Somali coastal resources and people's livelihoods? If so, are not the 'fish pirates' as culpable as the 'ship pirates' (you loot our fish, and we loot your ships)?

Following a proper understanding of this, more questions arise. Does the looting by the 'fish pirates' and the deprivation of people's livelihoods have anything to do with the emergence of the Al Shabaab? And then there are some questions on regional war and peace. Does the imposition of an order from outside Somalia in the form of Ethiopian, Kenyan and Ugandan troops, and the forcible removal of the Union of Islamic Courts that for a period brought some peace to Somalia in 2011–12, have anything to do with the continuing strife in the whole region? If so, are not Somalia's neighbouring countries as culpable as the feuding warlords of Somalia? Are the neighbouring countries fighting proxy wars on behalf of, for example, the United States in its relentless 'war on terror'? If so, are not the East African governments culpable for putting their innocent civilian populations at risk of violence?

These, I grant, are difficult questions. I pose them not rhetorically but to raise issues on which there is very little public debate outside of the African Union. Probably an interrogation of the discourse around Jubaland, Punt Land and Somaliland might have shed more light on some of these questions. Within the AU, there is also a need to discuss the Somalia issue against the larger geopolitical and economic context.

In late 2012, a former academic, Hassan Sheikh Mohamud, became president of Somalia. His election was hailed by the West: the US restored diplomatic ties after twenty years without them. The UN lifted the arms embargo under which the Western countries restricted arms deliveries to Somalia. In June 2013, Somalia joined the Cotonou Agreement (until then, it was not a member of the ACP group).[99] At the time, President Mohamud said that this would facilitate the national reconstruction process, as Somalia would be eligible to receive EU development aid.[100]

Fish is not the only Somali resource coveted by global corporations. Somalia also has oil. Clearly, President Mohamud was using oil as bait to attract foreign investment in fisheries and oil. In April 2014, Somalia signed a fisheries partnership agreement with the EU. Oil was a resource coveted by several competitors, among them the UK, France, Norway, Qatar and Turkey. Soon after Mohamud's election, British Prime Minister David Cameron hosted a conference on Somalia. Cameron said: 'We're helping to improve transparency and accountability by establishing a joint Financial Management Board, through which donors will work with the Somali government to make sure that revenue from key assets and international aid is used for the good of Somali people.'[101] The British put as its chief negotiator Lord Michael Howard, former leader of the British Conservative Party. He was appointed non-executive chairman of Soma Oil and Gas Exploration Limited, the Somalia-focused oil and gas company. In June 2014, under an investment agreement, the details of which are unclear, Soma announced that it had secured an offshore seismic acquisition agreement with Somalia: some 122,000 square kilometres of Somali coastline.[102]

Oil is used here only as an example. These 'resource wars' are waged throughout Africa, not just in relation to oil but also in relation to a vast amount of natural resources: diamonds, gold, iron, cobalt, uranium, copper, bauxite, silver, coffee, cocoa and wood. For example, the civil war in the Democratic Republic of Congo is linked not only with the smuggling of gold into Uganda and Rwanda, but also, and primarily, with the DRC's rich mineral resources, which are vital components for Western electronics and military industries.

GLOBAL ANARCHY: THE ABSENCE OF A CENTRALISED GLOBAL GOVERNANCE STRUCTURE

Global corporate competition is both conspiratorial and anarchic. Earlier, I referred to Al Jazeera's documentary *The Secret of Seven Sisters*, which shows how the Western oil cartel consisting of seven major oil corporations made a secret pact to control the world's oil. That is conspiratorial. There is a clear absence of any proper global governance structure that can regulate these global corporations.

The global financial system is also anarchic. What better authority than Hank Paulsen—who ended his long service as US Secretary of the Treasury during the financial crisis—to make this point? In an interview with the German newspaper *Handelsblatt* on 13 September 2013, he warned against another financial crisis, which could be triggered by one or more of the following factors:[103]

- The 'too big to fail banks': by 2013 the five biggest US banks had amassed $8.3 trillion in assets, $2.5 trillion more than in 2007;
- The ballooning derivatives market, which had grown from $586 trillion in 2007 to almost $633 trillion in 2013, and which was largely unregulated;
- Shadow banks: with assets of $67 trillion (growing rapidly), shadow banks comprise an unregulated banking sector that is not even subject to capital requirements.

I should add that there are some areas of global governance that work fairly well. But these are largely functional—'technical,' if you like—bodies, such as the International Telecommunication

Union and the World Meteorological Organisation. But when it comes to trade-related organisations such as the WTO, it is politics that is in command—the powerful dictate how the rules are made, interpreted and applied. On the other hand—and this is the anarchical aspect of the system—there are vast chunks of global governance matters which are left to corporations that are unregulated and conspiratorial, two aspects of the corporate world encased in the same toxic capsule.

As far as commodities are concerned, there is really no regulatory system. It must be understood that the speculators who deal in futures markets in commodity indexes have no interest in a monitoring system. In fact, because of the very nature of speculation in the commodities market, even the normal textbook rules of supply and demand do not apply. The speculators do not want commodities as an asset class to be related to other assets, such as equities, bonds, real estate or foreign exchange, for the whole point of 'hedging' is to play one set of odds against another. Since speculators have actually no interest in taking the physical delivery of commodities, they must sell the contracts before expiration—'short-selling'—and make room to buy new contracts. It is essentially an anarchic war system of trading.

In this system, the powerful rule, and the weak are subdued or sanctioned, as we saw in the previous chapter.

How, then, in this power-driven global anarchical 'system,' do we move from war to peace?

THE WORLD ON THE CUSP OF CIVILISATIONAL SHIFT

This is a vast and complex subject for a small book. However, I need to address it because I believe that trade war is only one dimension of a world that is drifting into a civilisational shift whose outlines are as yet only dimly perceived. In contrast to Francis Fukuyama's 'end of history' and Huntington's *clash of civilizations*,' I prefer to talk about *civilizational shift.*'[104]

My thesis is quite simple. The contemporary civilisational shift is based on three propositions.

ONE: No civilisation, however defined[105], lasts forever. Contrary to what most people think (or believe), so-called Western or capitalist civilisation is not everlasting. I share the sentiments of those who argue that this civilisation's callous exploitation of human labour and nature is finally coming to an end. It may take yet another century, but that is not really too long to wait. Civilisations previous to capitalism (such as the Aztec, Egyptian, Chinese, Indian and Persian civilisations) lasted much longer. Revolutions are part of the movement of history.

TWO: One might argue that if capitalism has not ended, it is because 'the end has not yet come.' Karl Marx thought that the international proletariat would be capitalism's nemesis. It might still be; we do not know. In the meantime, the Western brand of capitalism (with private property and the free market as its *raison d'etre*) is facing multiple nemeses, among them, in particular, the oppressed nations and cultures of the world. Recall Marx's memorable phrase in *The Communist Manifesto*: 'A spectre is haunting Europe—the spectre of communism. All the powers of old Europe have entered into a holy alliance to exorcise this spectre.'

THREE: This *Communist Manifesto* is dead. It is now *the spectre of the oppressed nations of the world (most significantly, the nationalism of the countries of the South) that is 'haunting Europe.'* And to be sure, all the powers of old Europe—led by the United States—have entered into an unholy alliance to 'exorcise this spectre.' This now is the new manifesto of our time: the *Manifesto of the Oppressed Nations and Exploited Peoples of the World.* There are two major manifestations of this spectre: national liberation and Islamic resurgence.

The National Liberation Movements

It is a strange parody of history and sociology that 'nationalism' is easier to explain than 'nation.' I will not go too much into the definitional issue. Some define 'nation' as a kind of 'cultural' identity; but then why did the Americans (who came largely from English or Irish stock) seek 'national liberation' from England? Is the US a 'nation'? But then where do you locate the 'nation of Islam' within the US? Do the people of 'Tanzania' constitute a 'nation'? But then do the people of Zanzibar constitute a separate nation?

The 'nation' is a theoretical abstraction whose vibrant energy is 'nationalism,' or 'national liberation,' where the key word is 'liberation.' People seek liberation—liberation from oppression and exploitation. People seek 'self-determination,' where the 'self' gets defined—and redefined—in the course of the struggle for liberation. Liberation is the constant motif; it is the self-identity that changes. I was born 'Ugandan' (of 'Indian' stock), but I am gradually 'evolving' towards becoming an 'East African.' The five 'states' (not 'nation states') of East Africa—Burundi, Rwanda, Tanzania, Kenya, and Uganda—were carved out by the colonialists a hundred or so years ago. In the chapter on Europe's trade war on Africa, we saw how these five countries are struggling to liberate themselves from the yoke of colonial-imperial rule, and possibly 'evolving' towards a new political entity called 'East Africa.' It is a process, not an event.[106]

The Foundations and Significance of Islamic Resurgence

The second manifestation of 'national liberation'—Islamic resurgence—is an even more complex phenomenon. I would argue that the foundations of this resurgence go back to the meteoric rise of Islam in the mid-seventh to mid-eleventh centuries, Islam's contribution to the European Enlightenment and Renaissance,[107] the Crusades, and the emergence of capitalism as a systematised mode of production in Europe.

Why the capitalist revolution did not come to the Islamic world (or for that matter to ancient India or ancient Meso-America) is of futile academic and speculative interest. The historical reality is that industrialisation and capitalism came first to Europe. Marx provided a vivid picture of 'primitive accumulation' that explained the basis of capitalism in England: the massive dispossession of the lands and property of the English and Irish peasantry (the so-called 'enclosure movement'), and the appropriation of the 'commons' by a rising landed gentry. This took place especially after the Black Death (c. 1348–50). Well before that, however, *the most colossal primitive accumulation took place during the Crusades,* which Marx missed in his analysis.

Eurocentric historians present the Crusades as Christian defensive wars against Islamic expansion on the frontiers of Europe, and as an effort to restore Christian access to holy places in and around Jerusalem. But this is only a part of the story. The Ottoman conquest of Eastern Europe had shaken the Christians. Then, for nearly two-hundred years—from 1030 onwards—the West sought, with much passion and rage, to reverse Islamic supremacy. If there was a World War I, this was the one—the Crusades.

At the end of the Crusades, one of the critical foundations for the West's advance towards capitalism was established: the creation of its financial center. During the Byzantine-Muslim War of 1030–35, the Italian city-state of Venice had weakened the Islamic hold on the Mediterranean Sea. The Normans, with the assistance of the Italian city-states of Genoa and Pisa, had retaken Sicily from the Muslims from 1061 to 1091. In the First Crusade (1095–99), the Crusaders seized Jerusalem, ending in the bloody slaughter of the Jews and Arabs who fought together against the Christians. In the Fourth Crusade (1202–04), Constantinople was attacked and its riches expropriated. This was the time of the Knights Templar financial innovations that tapped into the East's gold and silver hoards. The Fourth Crusade effectively resulted in the transfer of the monetary centre of the world from Byzantine and Arab lands to the West.[108]

Looking at that period from hindsight, this was a very significant development. Well before Columbus set sail to discover 'the East' in 1492, the West had established control over the emerging global money system—from the goldsmiths of Venice, to the Italian and Catalonia banking houses, to the German Hansa (warrior bands) and moneylenders (Weslers, Hoschstetters and Tuchmans), to the Hanseatic League and the formation of Europe's first major exchange in Brugge, to, finally, the creation in 1661 of the Bank of Sweden, the first Western bank of fiduciary issue, followed in 1694 by the creation of the Bank of England.[109]

However, in our own times, because of institutionalised racism and Islamophobia, this part of history is generally lost. Barring the more enlightened individuals, people in the West are socio-psychologically tuned to certain hubris about the 'higher' quality of Western civilisation as opposed to the 'lower' civilisations of Africa and the Orient. There is a commonly held perception (often because of trashy journalism) that the life or the human rights of an ordinary African, Afghan, Palestinian or Muslim is worth nothing compared to the life or rights of an ordinary 'white' person. This hubris poisons ordinary relations between the West and the Rest. This is the stark—and sad—reality of the contemporary postcolonial world.

If this is not understood, then nothing is understood about the rise of ISIS (Islamic State of Iraq and Syria).[110] The centuries-old feud between Shias and Sunnis remains a poignant factor, often fuelled by the West, which seeks to divide and rule the conquered people. The 'Wahhabisation' of Sunni Islam suited Western interests when they were fighting the Soviets in Afghanistan in the 1980s. The Empire has used the most reactionary atavistic throwbacks from the Islamic past to hit at third-world nationalists and progressive forces. ISIS itself is a product of NATO's attempt to force a regime change in Syria.

Anybody who values life, as well as liberty and security, can neither condone the West's imperial ambitions, nor Syria's dictatorial regime, nor the excesses of ISIS. Nobody in his or her right mind would condone the wanton brutality of ISIS's beheading of Western journalists and welfare workers. This cannot be accepted, even if the West or its agents did the same with Osama bin Laden, Sadaam Hussein, Muammar Gaddafi and countless others.

Nor should the actions of ISIS become the standard by which to judge other Islamic organisations, such as the Muslim Brotherhood—which, in any case, is not a monolithic organisation. One must not forget that in the 1930s the nationalist, anti-imperialist section of the Muslim Brotherhood played a vital role in India against the British Empire, to a point where Gandhi was in favour of the resurrection of the Caliphate. Today, of course, the Caliphate issue is a divisive one, even within the Islamic world.

The point is that unless one has a very long historical perspective, it is impossible to understand why moderate and secular Islam has been side-lined by militant, fundamentalist jihadists, why young Muslims from within the West join the ranks of the jihadists,[111] and why the command-and-control structure of NATO is a very different beast compared to the highly decentralised, self-recruited ISIS. How can one explain the resounding defeat, on 10 June 2014, of the NATO-supplied Iraqi army of 350,000 by ISIS fighters numbering no more than 1,300?[112] Whether ISIS succeeds in its ambitions—even partially—or whether NATO forces manage to defeat ISIS militarily, the seeds ISIS has planted will sprout again. The power of an idea—nourished as it is by the centuries-old history of the Crusades and the humiliation Muslims feel in their daily lives—cannot be brushed aside in a matter of years or decades.

THE THEORY AND PRACTICE OF REVOLUTIONARY CHANGE
The Mainstream Reformist Strategy: Whistling in the Dark
On 4 February 2014, Christine Lagarde, the head of the IMF, delivered the 2014 Richard Dimbleby Lecture in London.[113] In her speech, entitled 'A New Multilateralism for the Twenty-First Century,' she drew attention to many challenges facing the global system. She made a bold statement, with which I would generally agree:

> In the past, economists have underestimated the importance of inequality. They have focused on economic growth, on the size of the pie rather than its distribution. Today, we are more keenly aware of the damage done by inequality. Put simply, a severely skewed income distribution harms the pace and sustainability of growth over the longer term. It leads to an economy of exclusion, and a wasteland of discarded potential.

Among other things, she drew attention to 'a shift in global power from West to East and from North to South.' This is, of course, relative, because she would agree that the North is extraordinarily powerful militarily. Let us search Google and see what it says. I (to use an awful modernist term) googled 'US military compared to the rest of the world,' and this is what I got: 'The U.S. spent more on defence in 2012 than the countries with the next ten highest budgets combined. The $682 billion spent by the U.S. in 2012, according to the Office of Management and Budget, was more than the combined military spending of China, Russia, the United Kingdom, Japan, France, Saudi Arabia, India, Germany, Italy and Brazil — which spent $652 billion, according to the SIPRI Military Expenditure Database.'[114]

In her speech, Lagarde gave a menu of things that needed to be done in order to change the situation for the better. Among these she mentioned 'immediate priority for growth to go beyond the financial crisis,' dealing with 'high private and public debt,' 'structural impediments to competitiveness and growth,' 'weak bank systems,' and the need for 'a finance system that serves productive economy—in which industry takes co-responsibility.' She ended her speech with a challenge to the present generation: 'Our forefathers vanquished the demons of the past, bequeathing to us a better world—and our generation was the main beneficiary . ... Now it is our turn to pave the way for the next generation. Are we up to the challenge? Our future depends on the answer to that question.'

This is essentially Western strategy to save a world in crisis. Understandably, the head of the IMF could not have advanced a revolutionary strategy, even if in her private moments she might have thought of one.

The chances of Christine Lagarde's wish list getting implemented are, to be candid, practically zero. 'The demons of the past' are here to stay, until the final demise of capitalism and imperialism. I do not wish to belabour the point. The world will continue to grow in the material sense, for sure, because of (to use a Marxist expression) the ceaseless development of 'productive forces' under capitalism.[115] For our purposes what is significant is that the distribution of the fruits of human labour under capitalism (to put it at its simplest) is skewed in favour of the rich and against the poor within and between nations. *The capitalist-imperialist system polarises wealth and poverty. It is within its DNA.* If the working classes have gained something—materially and in terms of having a voice in the 'capitalist democracies' (really, plutocracies), then it has been as a result of resistance at the political level. The world has become more unequal over the last 50 years than over the preceding one thousand. The OECD's 2011 study—*'Divided we Stand: Why Inequality Keeps Rising'*—revealed that globally the rich-poor gap has widened in the last decade. Between nations this is clearly evident. But even within advanced countries—including the 'egalitarian' states such as Germany, Denmark and Sweden—the rich-poor income and welfare gap is growing[116].

There is no possibility of a 'distributive solution' within the present system, which is structurally engineered to produce inequality. And this is where Christine Lagarde's optimism crashes to the ground.

In contrast to this reformist strategy, what we offer is a strategy of guerrilla war against imperial peace.

A GUERRILLA WAR AGAINST IMPERIAL PEACE

Trade war is not the same as military war; they are different in significant ways. But there are certain principles of military warfare that could apply to trade war. An asymmetric power situation demands guerrilla tactics. There is a lot to learn from, among others, Sun Tzu, Mao, Che Guevara, Cabral, Le Duan, Giap, Gandhi, Nkrumah, Nyerere, and Castro.[117] You might be surprised that I have put all the above in the same group, but if you look at their lives and how they fought against asymmetrical power situations, you will understand that they left behind a rich legacy of strategy and tactics for engaging in struggle against more powerful and dangerous adversaries.

Why a Nonviolent Guerrilla War?

The first question I face is whether I'm serious about a 'guerrilla war.' Am I being hyperbolic, even paranoid? Or just romantic?

The strategy I present is not romantic. It is not paranoid either. It is serious. We have a lot to learn from Che, the emblematic guerrilla fighter, but we need to go beyond him. Those who are looking for another kind of peace have no choice but to engage in a nonviolent guerrilla war against the present order. I say nonviolent because I firmly believe that whilst it may be slow-moving, nonviolent struggle it is more humane, more effective, and more lasting. Violence is divisive, and whilst its outcome may be almost immediate, it can be less enduring. There are many challenges facing nonviolent guerrilla struggles. The journey 'from here to there' (however one defines the 'there') has immediate tactical challenges that may have to be addressed here and now, but strategically, it is a long and protracted struggle.

A protracted struggle is not a one-day wonder. Those for whom the root cause of all contemporary problems is capitalism face an epochal struggle. They may have to wait a long time. For sure, the system is cracking—like we observed when tracking the present anarchic financial mess—but the capitalist ship is not about to disintegrate. And there are over six billion people on board. The strategy is to build a thousand—a hundred thousand—boats and begin tossing them into the ocean so that 'women and children' accompanied by good oarsmen begin to set forth in the bumpy sea. By the time the capitalist ship sinks, there should be nobody on board. So yes, it is an epochal struggle, and it already began with the Russian Revolution in 1917—if not even earlier. Between then and now, various experiments at socialism have been attempted. These have left behind debris of lost or cracked boats in the ocean, but they have also left a wealth of experience and knowledge. Humanity has to learn from the successes and failures of nearly a century of struggles against capitalism and its necessary out-growth, imperialism.

This is a difficult, complex subject to tackle in the conclud-ing section of a book that deals with a small aspect of the impe-rial ship's doomed destiny. So I give below only a glimpse of the bigger picture. Without the bigger strategic vision, the tactical responses on the trade issue might not be only misguided, but also illusory.

The Philosophy of Contradictions

Many guerrilla movements have used Mao's teachings—including his theory of contradictions—for legitimate political ends. Some such movements—such as those in Peru and Sri Lanka—have ended with disastrous consequences for leaders and people alike. I was part of an underground Maoist guerrilla movement in Uganda in the 1970s and '80s, and I have some experiential knowledge of its strengths and weaknesses. Therefore, while we have a lot to learn from Mao, we need to go beyond him.

In going beyond Mao, I widen the scope to include bigger issues of philosophy. The following diagram is an aid to explaining the complexity and interconnectedness of its three aspects.

As explained earlier, I would say that at the material level the most dynamic forces are the development of the productive forces.[118] Following Marx and Mao, I would say that the working classes—those working on land and in industry and services—are the most revolutionary classes. However, I would add that it is not simply the working classes that constitute the 'masses.' Following Moses, Christ, the Prophet Mohammad, Guru Nanak, Gandhi, Nyerere, and Mandela, among others, I would say that the 'masses' is a much bigger concept. I would also say that the masses are inspired not only by material forces, i.e., the experience of oppression and exploitation at the level of production. They are also inspired by what, for lack of a better word, I call 'spiritual forces.' These include, in my definition, ideology and the zeitgeist (the spirit of the age). I would add, however, that I identify the zeitgeist not as 'modernisation' or 'globalisation,' but as resistance against exploitation and oppression at all levels—nation, class, gender, age, religion and the environment.

I realise that I am treading on a hazardous philosophical terrain, and I am no philosopher. You might have problems with my above philosophy. But I leave it at that. My aim is to stir imagination,

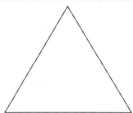

PHILOSOPHY OF CONTRADICTIONS

Conservative forces at the international and national levels

Dynamic productive forces   **Revolutionary social forces**

not with a view to reaching a consensus, but to generate a healthy debate. This should traverse not only strategic and tactical issues but also normative and ethical issues.

One question still remains. Marx and Mao envisaged a socialist vision. What, you might ask, is my vision? Well, building on my capitalist ship analogy, my vision consists of thousands of small boats in the ocean—thousands of nonviolent, more or less self-reliant communities that organise their own methods of production and consumption. These communities should not only be 'other-conscious,' but also 'nature-conscious.' They should trade among themselves for goods and services which they do not have the resources to produce, but they should 'trade' in them as 'use values' and not as commoditised 'exchange values.' To paraphrase Gandhi, the world has enough to satisfy the basic needs of all, but not the greed of a billion consumers at the cost of the five billion who are dispossessed and disempowered, nor at the cost of the environment and other species. Humanity should embrace all beings, including flora and fauna.

And now to the gargantuan question: how do we transform this vision into reality? Transforming vision into reality is easier said than done. But we have to begin somewhere. There is no other way if we are to move out of the grossly unjust and violent 'imperial peace' to a new kind of peace, 'peoples' peace.'

Mobilising Material and Social Forces
Referring to the triangular relationship sketched above, we need reflection and action on two levels:

a) At the material level—that of production and exchange;
b) At the social level—that of relations of production, and the ideological and moral basis of society.

The following are preliminary thoughts, given the limited space and the need to convey a sense of direction as briefly as possible.

At the material level: 'decoupling'

In 1990, Samir Amin wrote an influential book—*Delinking Towards a Polycentric World*. Amin has been a major figure in challenging the existing capitalist and imperial order, and in providing a generation of scholars—from the North as well the South—thoughtful and compelling arguments on why a new order is unavoidable. Capitalism has come to the end of its road, he argued, and humanity needs to move towards a new civilisation.[119]

My decoupling concept is similar to Amin's 'delinking.' Amin uses it primarily as a prescriptive concept; I use it descriptively as well as prescriptively. In other words, I argue that decoupling is already taking place. I will return to this, once I distance the idea from similar nuanced versions of 'delinking,' even when the word itself is not employed. Thus, for example, Joseph Stiglitz nuanced it in his essay 'On the Wrong Side of Globalization on Trans-Pacific Partnership.'[120] Stiglitz is right (in my view) to critique the TPP, but he seems to suggest that there is a 'right side' to 'globalization.' In essence, Stiglitz is in the Christian Laggard reformist mould, and therefore has the same illusions as Laggard when it comes to reforming the capitalist system by delinking from its 'free market' version to some kind of 'regulated capitalism.'[121]

I start with the proposition that *capitalism is unregulatable*. It is essentially anarchic; and its major players—the transnational corporations and financial and commodity speculators—prefer an anarchic system which they can manipulate. Some mainstream economists and journalists—like Wolfgang Munchau and David Pilling—have argued, in essence, that globalisation is real and here to stay and that decoupling from it is not possible. To them I would say that decoupling is not only possible, but already happening, even within the capitalist framework. The globalisation project is in a deep systemic crisis. Countries like China, India, Brazil, Chile, Malaysia, Venezuela, etc., have partially decoupled from the global system—for example, defying the IMF by refusing to liberalise capital flows; putting in place full (China) or partial (India, Argentina) control over their currencies; and refusing to buckle under liberalising pressures from the US, the EU and the WTO. They have done relatively well in providing 'fire wall' protection against the viral attack triggered by the US housing crisis in 2007–08. This has created policy space for China, India, Brazil and Russia, enabling them to withstand the financial crisis much better than the North.[122] In other words, to continue with my ship analogy, these countries—the BRICS, plus Venezuela, Chile, Malaysia, and Iran, among others—have kept themselves in the capitalist ship but are not obeying the captain's command, and have put into the ocean their own little capitalist boats to decouple from the main ship.

In my dictionary, then, 'regionalism' is also a kind of decoupling. We have seen in chapter three that the people (as distinct from the Governments) of East Africa have (so far) been able to sustain their regionalist ambition and programme, and have refused to knuckle under the European Union's divide and rule tactics.

I would go one step further. Whilst countries seek decoupling from globalisation, the Empire forcibly decouples 'difficult' countries like Russia, China, Cuba and many others. Following the Ukraine crisis in 2012, the West imposed sanctions on Russia which amounted, in effect, to decoupling Russia from globalisation. In other words, decoupling—not integrating into Empire-led globalisation—is the zeitgeist of our time.

From exchange values to use values

A more radical form of decoupling is one that delinks societies from the capitalist system of commodity production. That is indeed the long-term strategy, the vision for the future. I argue that at the local or community level, ordinary people have to make a *conscious* effort to create ways of decoupling from the iniquitous market-based value system.

At the heart of the contemporary civilisational crisis is the reductionist logic that values everything in terms of money. Everything, including the dignity of the individual—especially vulnerable women and children—is subject to the 'law of value.' Everything is commoditised. However, in the interstices of this globalised system there are heroic efforts by some communities to distance themselves from the system. There are many innovative approaches, including the production of goods and services based on exchange that doesn't involve money. Also, where money is needed as a medium of exchange, communities have created 'communal money' (a kind of labour voucher system) that is delinked from national currencies, notoriously subject to fluctuations and speculation.[123]

At the social level: the role of ideology and knowledge

The German philosopher Karl Mannheim defined ideology as the total system of thought held by society's ruling groups. Ideology obscures real conditions and thereby preserves the status quo. In his classic *Ideology and Utopia: An Introduction to the Sociology of Knowledge*, he analyzed the relationship between sociology and social policy, and the role of the intelligentsia.[124] Borrowing from Marx, Mannheim argued that the ideological structure of thought is conditioned by the class structure of society. He went on to say that in class-divided societies a special stratum of individuals 'whose only capital consist[s] in their education' develop their ideas to advance the interests of different classes. Amongst them are those that serve the ruling classes; they provide the knowledge that forms the kernel of the ruling ideology, the dominant '*Weltanschauung.*' These are opposed by another stratum that challenges the ruling orthodoxy, including the production of knowledge. Mannheim argued that the prevailing ideology makes the ruling groups opposed to knowledge that would threaten their continued domination.

Following Mannheim, I argue that we are at a crossroad between, on the one hand, the neoclassical theory that has ruled for nearly forty years and that has produced the failed ideology of neoliberalism, and on the other hand, the challenge that the radical intelligentsia faces to produce knowledge that would liberate the people as well as their political leaders from the prevailing obscurantist mindset.

The question of where knowledge comes from and how do we know what we know has occupied philosophers for centuries. One of the finest books I have read on the subject in recent time is Nassim Taleb's *The Black Swan* in which, among other things, he attacks 'decontextualized knowledge' (or what he calls 'Platonicity').[125] From an African perspective, Dani Wadada Nabudere, the Ugandan scholar and political activist with whom I worked for close to thirty years, wrote some of his reflections on this subject just before his death in November 2011. In his two books *Afrikology: Philosophy and Wholeness: An Epistemology*, and *Afrikology and Transdisciplinarity: A Restorative Epistemology*, Nabudere analyses the crisis created by the Cartesian fragmentation of knowledge in the West, and offers insights from the African traditional knowledge systems.[126]

Beyond the ideological level (which I define here mainly in the realm of economics) is the struggle at the political, moral and ethical level. The Universal Declaration of Human Rights is a good example. The Declaration is based on principles and values that most of us would endorse. But in the realm of global politics, given its basically anarchist character, human rights have been grossly abused by NATO countries to intervene in the domestic affairs of mainly the countries of the South. One of its most abused corollaries is the Responsibility to Protect (R2P) resolution of the United Nations (resolution A/RES/63/308).[127]

It is the same with other valued norms such as democracy, freedom of the press, good governance and others. They have become normative tools to fight what amounts to a war against the countries of the South, such as Iran and Cuba, or against groups within these countries in the name of rooting out the 'terrorists.' It is necessary to create a different world without NATO and similar military alliances. Then, these political and ethical norms would mean what they genuinely stand for.

FROM HERE TO THERE: A THOUSAND BOATS ON THE OCEAN

On how to move forward, let us listen to the Chinese sage and military strategist Sun Tzu (544–496 BC), who drew his wisdom from Taoism, the knowledge that fostered both the healing arts and the martial arts in China. His classic *The Art of War* is full of wisdom on warfare that could well apply to our own time, and all forms of war, including guerrilla war.[128] It should be on the desk of every guerrilla fighter. Sun Tzu says that according to the rule of military operations, there are nine kinds of grounds:

1. *The ground of dissolution*: where local interests fight amongst themselves on their own territory;
2. *Light ground*: when you enter others' land, but not deeply;
3. *The ground of contention*: land that would be advantageous to you if you got it, and to opponents if they got it;

4. *Trafficked ground:* land where you and others can come and go;
5. *Intersecting ground:* land surrounded on three sides by competitors, with access to all people in the continent;
6. *Heavy ground:* when you enter deeply into others' land, past many cities and towns;
7. *Bad ground:* when you traverse mountain forests, steep defiles, marshes or routes difficult to travel;
8. *Surrounded ground:* when the way in is narrow and the way out difficult. Even a small enemy force can strike you;
9. *Dying ground:* where you will survive if you fight quickly and perish if you do not.[129]

Sun Tzu gives detailed strategies and tactics for each ground. 'So let there be no battle on a ground of dissolution, let there be no stopping on light ground,' and so on. He is opposed to war: 'To win without fighting is best . . . . A victorious army first wins and then seeks battle; a defeated army first battles and then seeks victory.'

If I were to summarise *Trade is War* in terms of the above, I would say that imperialism has managed to push the South onto '*bad ground.*' Some countries, like China, Cuba, and Iran, are united in the face of the adversaries, but most others are on the '*ground of dissolution.*' This is mainly an outcome of the divide-and-rule tactics of imperialist powers, who, despite their differences, close ranks under NATO when faced with situations like Libya in 2011 and Ukraine in 2014, and Palestine since the founding of the state of Israel in 1949. The war over EPAs waged between Europe and Africa shows that Africa is on the '*ground of dissolution,*' and unless Africa unites, it will soon find itself on '*dying ground.*' Africa's industries will simply perish, and with them Africa's future. But this is no reason to despair or give up. The UN Security Council is more or less paralyzed, but Russia and China's veto power can save the South from being pushed onto. The General Assembly has no sanctions power, but it is trafficked ground. It is also '*surrounded ground*' a '*ground of contention,*' and can be a useful means of isolating the adversary, as Palestine has done in relation to Israel. Also, the UN provides a useful platform to know your enemies and your friends, and to form alliances. As Sun Tzu says: 'Those who do not know the plans of competitors cannot prepare alliances.'

Tzu says: 'When your strategy is deep and far-reaching you can win before you even fight.'

It is time to strategise for launching a thousand boats into the ocean. This is where I stand.

ENDNOTES

1   These quotes are from my notes taken at the meeting.

2   See glossary of terms.

3   As quoted by Alex Smith of the Associated Press, San Francisco, 26 October 2008.

4   The term 'Washington Consensus' refers generally to a set of market-based economic policy prescriptions (also referred to as 'neoliberal fundamentalism' by its critics) enforced by the World Bank, the IMF, and Western countries in return for so-called 'development aid' to developing countries.

5   Neo-Keynesian economics is a school of macroeconomic thought that was developed in the post-Second World War period from the writings of John Maynard Keynes. The theory questions the dominant monetarist macroeconomic thought enshrined in the Washington Consensus.

6   My own view on this is based on the fact that international society is an acephalous society—like the precolonial Karamojong in Uganda where I grew up. An acephalous community is 'stateless'; it has no centralised authority. The world, too, has no centralised authority. The United Nations is an assembly of nations; it is not a 'world state.' Its decisions are reached on the basis of negotiations between sovereign states, who surrender their will to a collective process only as much as they wish to or are coerced to. The big and powerful make most of the 'wishes' and the weak and vulnerable by and large accept their diktat because they are 'coerced' to. But this realpolitik perspective of international relations also does not entirely correspond with the reality on the ground. In between 'muscle flexing' among the 'big and powerful' there is a time-honoured practice of diplomacy. Diplomacy seeks to work out negotiated arrangements short of war. My own view (philosophical or jurisprudential—whatever one calls it) is that in an acephalous society the language of diplomacy is preferable to that of sanctions.

7   There is one school of judicial activists that says that WTO decisions create 'precedents' that over time 'evolve' into a 'system of norms' through customary practice and habitual obedience. I will not get into this teleological Hegelian-Kantian perspective which I do not share, but which is resurgent among the 'left' in parts of continental Europe. For more on this, see '*Kantian Tradition*' in Martin Griffiths (1999, 2006), *Fifty Key Thinkers in International Relations,* Routledge.

8   I have borrowed this phrase from Hudec, see note x.

9   The first set is subject to Section 301 of the 1988 Omnibus Trade & Competitiveness Act, and the second is subject to anti-dumping and countervailing duties (CVDs).

10 For an excellent discussion on the concept of 'fairness' in international trade, see Robert E. Hudec (1990), '*Mirror, Mirror on the wall: The concept of fairness in US Foreign Trade Policy,*' in his (1999), *Essays on the Nature of International Trade law,* Cameron.

11 The Kyoto Protocol to the United Nations Framework Convention on Climate Change (UNFCCC) is a legally binding international treaty with the goal of preventing dangerous anthropogenic (human-induced) interference in the climate system. It imposes binding obligations on industrialised countries to reduce emissions of greenhouse gases.

12 'Will you walk into my parlour,' said the Spider to the Fly. 'The way into my parlour is up a winding stair.' 'Oh no, no,' said the little Fly, 'to ask me is in vain, for who goes up your winding stair can ne'er come down again.'

13 Subsequently, I wrote a story on this titled '*My Attempt to Enter the Boiler Room at Doha Ministerial,*' see *SEATINI Bulletin*, 30 November 2001.

14 By contrast, at the Sixth WTO Ministerial in Hong Kong, there was no 'consensus' in this technical sense. On the last day the chairman of the conference read out the 'Hong Kong declaration,' which only a few privileged delegations had seen. Without further discussion, the chairman hit the gavel on the table and announced that since nobody had raised objections, the declaration was adopted by consensus. Immediately, from the floor arose the heads of the delegations of Cuba and Venezuela to raise objections. But when the chairman did not recognise them, they rushed to the podium and protested to the chairman that they had not agreed to the declaration. The Cuban-Venezuelan objections were duly 'noted' in the records. I was at the meeting, so later I asked a legal expert from the WTO

what the legal consequences were of this withdrawal of consent by the two countries. He said, 'Nothing. They are small players. They don't count.'

15 However, see the previous note.

16 The Dependencia Theory is based on the argument that poor states are impoverished and rich ones enriched by the way poor states are integrated into the world system of production and exchange. The theory states that resources flow from the 'periphery' of poor and underdeveloped economies to the 'center' of the global system of wealthy countries. This, the theory argues, is the root cause of the continuing and increasing gap between rich and poor nations.

17 See chapter three, 'EPAs: Europe's Trade War on Africa.'

18 See Ziegler, Jean (2011). *The Fight for the Right to Food*: Lessons Learnt, Palgrave. The book argues for a 'right to food in theory and in practice,' based on conceptual and legal developments and experiences in eleven countries across Africa, Asia and Latin America.

19 I can vouch for this because I've seen this first-hand in the 1980s and 1990s when working in the rural areas of Zimbabwe as a 'development consultant'

20 Agricultural Subsidies in the WTO Green Box, ICTSD, September 2009.

21 See South Centre, Analytical Note 'Present Situation of the WTO Doha Talks and Comments on the 21 April Documents,' April 2011.

22 Oxfam, 2003.'*Cultivating Poverty: The Impact of US Cotton Subsidies on Africa*,' briefing paper; Baffes, 2003.

23 Andrea R. Woodward (2007). Case Study #10-5, '*The Impact of U.S. Subsidies on West African Cotton Production*.' In: Per Pinstrup-Andersen and Fuzhi Cheng (editors), '*Food Policy for Developing Countries: Case Studies*.' http://cip.cornell.edu/dns.gfs/1200428204.

24 See IFDC: '*Linking Cotton and Food Security in the Cotton-Four (C-4) Countries*,' *IFDC Report* Volume 38, No. 1 (2013). http://www.ifdc.org/About/IFDC_Articles/Linking-Cotton-and-Food-Security-in-the-Cotton-Four/

25 Ibid.

26 For an account of how the MDGs got into the UN agenda, and the role played by 'high fliers' in the Western charity and media world such as Bob Geldof, Bono, George Clooney and Angelina Jolie, see Sumner, Andy and Meera Tiwari (2009). *After 2015: International Development Policy at a Crossroads*, Palgrave.

27 *South Bulletin* #73, 7 July 2013.

28 See www.businesseurope.eu.

29 Robert Skidelsky (2000). *John Maynard Keynes, Vol. 3: Fighting for Britain, 1937–1946*, McMillan.

30 Ibid.

31 African soldiers carried the essential supplies—just like in the old slave-trade period—and were called Carrier Corps. This is where the main market in Dar es Salaam got its name—*Kariako*—whose origin is hardly known to the present generation of African people.

32 Dani Nabudere (1980). *Imperialism and Revolution in Uganda*, Onyx Press, p. 87.

33 http://en.wikipedia.org/wiki/Lend-Lease

34 See L.C. Gardner (1964). *Economic Aspects of New Deal Diplomacy*, Madison, 1964, p. 272–91.

35 Few people remember that an initial plan was the so-called Morgenthau Plan that advocated measures to destroy Germany's industrial capacity to wage war and reduce it to an agricultural country. It is not farfetched to suggest, following Erik Reinert, that what the West is doing in Africa is applying a version of the Morgenthau and not Marshall Plan. This time, however, the idea is not to destroy Africa's capacity to wage war but to reduce it to an agricultural region for the industrialising countries of the West. In his review of Paul Collier's *The Bottom Billion: Why the Poorest Countries are Failing and What Can Be Done About It*, Reinert writes: 'When the Allies wanted to punish Germany after the Second World War the cruellest plan . . . was forced deindustrialisation: the Morgenthau Plan. This plan was, however, so effective in producing mass poverty that it only lasted two years and was replaced by the Marshall Plan, a plan for re-industrialisation. This point was completely lost to development economics under neoliberalism . . . . In this longer term perspective, the de-industrialisation caused by the neoliberalist shock therapy—a modern Morgenthau Plan—will increasingly be seen as a folly. Putting Paul Collier, the former chief economist of the World Bank and one of the architects of this folly, in charge of explaining what went wrong with globalisation is akin to putting Attila the Hun in charge of the Ministry of Roman Reconstruction. Collier's book contains more attempts to cover up the past than to present new constructive insights, and more descriptions of symptoms

of poverty than of its root causes.' See Erik S. Reinert (2005) '*Development and Social Goals: Balancing Aid and Development to Prevent Welfare Colonialism,*' The Other Canon Foundation, Norway & Tallinn University of Technology, Estonia.

36 See Jeffrey Sachs (2009). *Common Wealth*, Penguin.

37 See also Richard N. Gardner (1956). *Sterling-Dollar Diplomacy,* Clarendon Press.

38 It is commonplace for economists to compare, for example, Ghana with Malaysia. The latter has become a 'middle-income' country, and Ghana remains more or less where it was in 1957. But the two situations are very different. Africa was tied, hand and foot, to colonial appendages—such as the imperial 'preference' and currency systems, and to imperial structures of governance. By contrast, largely because of the influence of the Chinese Revolution in 1949, some of the East Asian countries took a more radical, revolutionary approach. Other countries—like South Korea and Taiwan—were able to exploit the threat of Communism to extract from the US and Europe major concessions on trade, investments and transfer of technology.

39 Charles E. Harahan (2001). '*The U.S.-European Union Banana Dispute,*' Congressional Research Service, The Library of Congress, United States. Also, Hans-Peter Werner, '*Lomé, the WTO, and bananas,*' in *The Courier ACP-EU* No. 166, November–December 1997: p. 59–60.

40 See chapter two for an explanation of green- and blue-box measures.

41 Nabudere had been teaching a course in the law faculty of the university on the legal aspects of international trade and had studied this subject in some detail. He asked me to accompany him to a meeting with Ramphal at the Kilimanjaro Hotel, to argue against signing the Lomé Convention. Ramphal listened to us politely and agreed with us in principle, but he said we had to be practical. In those days there were no NGOs of the kind we have today, and so Nabudere and I were whistle-blowing in the wilderness. Our voices could be easily dismissed as academic.

42 Dani Nabudere (1979). Lom. Convention and the Crisis of Neo-colonialism: An Evaluation of Lom. I–III in *Essays on the Theory and Practice of Imperialism.* Onyx.

43 It is interesting that all postcolonial trade agreements between Africa and Europe were signed in former French colonies in Africa—Yaoundé in the

Cameroun, Lomé in Togo, and Cotonou in Benin. Compared to the giant states of Africa—the Congo, Nigeria and South Africa—these are puny states. Why these small francophone countries, and not the large states of Africa, were selected as places to sign agreements that are so significant for African-European relations is a question that I leave for readers to speculate about.

44 For those more technical- or legal-minded readers, I would suggest the many documents put out by the South Centre from a southern perspective. One of these is 'EPAs and WTO Compatibility: Developing Country Perspective,' informal note, 11 August 2010. Good coverage from the other side as it were (that is, from a European perspective) can be found in Sanoussi Bilal (2007). 'Concluding EPA Negotiations: Legal and Institutional Issues,' ECDPM.

45 Once again, the reality has changed since around 2008—with the global financial and economic crisis, and the considerable disillusionment with the EU among ordinary voters in most EU countries

46 See www.businesseurope.eu.

47 See 'EPA Negotiations: African Countries Continental Review' (www.uneca.org/publications/no-64-epa-negotiations-african-countries-continental-review). Europe's divide-and-rule tactics make it difficult for different sub-regions or countries to push back on an agreement that creates the 'dying ground' for Africa. The phrase 'dying ground' is from Sun Tzu, the ancient Chinese War Strategist. For a more detailed discussion on Sun Tzu, see the last chapter.

48 'Terms of Trade' refers to the relative price of exports in terms of imports. Simply put, it means the amount of import goods a country can purchase per unit of export goods. A deterioration of a country's terms of trade (as generally is the case with African countries) means that it can buy less imports for any given amount of exports. It also means its workers have to work harder to import the same amount of goods.

49 It is important to add here that whilst these were the issues that concerned us in East Africa in 2010, they are still contentious and not settled. The EC continued to insist on these demands; it added the threat of cuts in its so-called 'development aid' to East Africa. It has also threatened Kenya by saying that, as a non-LDC, it would lose preference in the European market, thus encouraging the big transnational producers and export-

ers of flowers based in Kenya to put pressure on the government to sign the FEPA. Timothy Clarke, the head of the European Union Delegation in Tanzania, said that the EU was East Africa's single largest market and that Kenya would be the biggest loser if the talks collapsed because it lacked alternative means to trade with Europe upon closure of the preferential window. As a non-member of the Highly Indebted Poor Country (HIPC), a collapse of the talks would force Kenya to trade with the EU on the less generous General System of Preferences (GSP) platform. That meant the country's exports that entered the European market on zero tariffs would start attracting duty of between 8.5 per cent and 15.7 per cent. For good measure, he added that the loss of tariff preferences with the shift to GSP would cost Kenya investments worth $700 million and thousands of jobs in the horticulture sector. See *Business Daily* (Nairobi), 9 June 2010. It should be obvious that Clarke was simply doing his job. He was using threats and scare tactics to influence Kenya government's position on EPA. As I have recounted in the body of this chapter, Kenya loses more by signing the EPA than by not signing it. Why Kenya proceeded to sign the EPA is a question that historians must answer. In the relationship between the Empire and a neo-colony, much goes on behind the scene that is not visible at first sight.

50   Kenya Human Rights Commission (2010). *Possible Impact on Human Rights of the Framework for the Economic Partnership Agreements (EPAs) Between the East African Community and the European Union.*

51   See CTA Brussels Newsletter, 08 April 2011, www.cta.int.

52   The above-quoted *Business Daily* of 9 June 2010 had reported that the statements for CSOs in Tanzania and another for Uganda signed by the Southern and Eastern Africa Trade Information and Negotiation Institute (SEATINI) in Kampala, were distributed at the venue of the meeting. Both statements had observed that East Africa was not ready for free trade with Europe: 'The massive difference in the size of our economies, that has been historically created, will not result in mutually beneficial trade, it will mean further European domination. In the light of this, we need to maintain the right to use tariffs and other interventions to develop our existing and new industries in the future.' The statement cautioned that 'free trade' which Europe was calling for 'was not in fact free at all and was certainly not fair, arguing that Europe spends hundreds of billions of

Euros supporting their farmers and are not willing to change or negotiate that stand. These subsidies lead to dumping of cheap products in our markets threatening the livelihoods of farmers. It also makes it very difficult to compete in Europe against the local subsidised production.'

53 At the 2003 WTO Cancun Ministerial I was a representative of the civil society in the official delegation of Uganda led by Minister Edward Rugumayo. The African Union had taken a collective stand against certain positions taken by the US and the EU, especially on Agriculture. Rugumayo had of course taken the AU position. Within hours of the opening of the conference, the Minister received a faxed message from President Museveni instructing him to distance himself from the AU position. Later we learnt from reliable sources that the President had been 'requested' by the US not to challenge the AU-EU position at the Ministerial. Museveni was no 'push-over'; he could stand up to the Empire if his interests were at stake. On this particular occasion that he must have decided that it was probably not worth challenging the Empire.

54 The deadline for withdrawing the market access regulation 'MAR 1528' was established three years earlier. MAR 1528 provided duty-free, quota-free (DFQF) market access to ACP countries.

55 Yash Tandon (1988). *Ending Aid Dependence*, South Centre. Also Yash Tandon (2012). *Demystifying Aid*, Pambazuka Insights.

56 'If nature has made any one thing less susceptible than all others of exclusive property, it is the action of the thinking power called an idea, which an individual may exclusively possess as long as he keeps it to himself; but the moment it is divulged, it forces itself into the possession of everyone, and the receiver cannot dispossess himself of it. Its peculiar character, too, is that no one possesses the less, because every other possesses the whole of it. He who receives an idea from me, receives instruction himself without lessening mine; as he who lights his taper at mine, receives light without darkening me.' Thomas Jefferson, Letter to Isaac McPherson, August 13, 1813. See http://en.wikipedia.org/wiki/Intellectual_property.

57 The European Pirate Parties members are mainly the youth. They are children of the digital revolution, and their main concerns are with free software, especially music, and the reform of the copyright and the patent system. Of late they appear to have given up on issues like seeds and genes.

Nonetheless, they are potential allies in the South's war on global intellectual property regimes.

58 Ibn al-Khatib provided empirical evidence that the Black Death in Europe spread through contagion rather than a result of a religious curse, as the contemporary Europeans thought. Other scientific scholars included the physicians al-Razi Rhazes and al-Haytham. The English historian Arnold Toynbee, in his classic *A Study of History* (1955, OUP), was one of the few European historians of integrity who recognised the role Islam played in bringing science and enlightenment to Europe.

59 http://en.wikipedia.org/wiki/International_Assessment_of_Agricultural_Knowledge,_Science_and_Technology_for_Development

60 See WHO A/CEWG/3, 2 November 2012, www.who.int/phi/1-cewg-secretariat_paper-en.pdf?ua=1.

61 Information from my notes based on an interview with the Chinese ambassador in Geneva, 14 January 2009. Thus, whilst the Chinese government accepts the WIPO and WTO norms on intellectual property, and from time to time reins in local companies that violate these norms, it also turns a blind eye to what the West calls the 'piracy' of their intellectual property.

62 This became a major issue between the US and Germany in early 2014 when the Germans uncovered an American industrial espionage network.

63 This refers to the famous dystopian novel by George Orwell, *1984*, with 'Big Brother' constantly watching the movements of citizens. Although that setting was national, we have now entered its global dimension.

64 One report suggested that the adoption of open-source software models has resulted in savings of about $60 billion per year to consumers. See Richard Rothwell (2008). 'Creating wealth with free software,' *Free Software Magazine*.

65 This refers to a movement in England in 1811 to 1817 when artisans smashed machinery to replace it with low-wage, low-skill labourers. The term 'Luddites' has since then been used, popularly, to malign anybody who is opposed to global corporate controlled innovation.

66 Gandhi: 'A country remains poor in wealth, both materially and intellectually, if it does not develop its handicrafts and its industries and lives a lazy parasitic life by importing all the manufactured articles from outside . . . . We are dependent upon the outside world for most manufactured

goods . . . . But in giving a definition care had to be taken not to make the definition so narrow as to make manufacture all but impossible or so wide as to become farcical and Swadeshi only in name.' *Young India*, 20 August 1931.

67 '*Nganga*' A Bantu term for an herbalist or spiritual healer in many African societies and also in many societies of the African diaspora, such as those in Brazil.

68 There is a huge amount of documented evidence to support this. See, for example, George Susan (1976), *How the Other Half Dies: The Real Reasons for World Hunger*, Penguin; Vandana Shiva (1992), *The Violence of the Green Revolution: Ecological Degradation and Political Conflict in Punjab*, Zed Press; and Vandana Shiva (2000), *Stolen Harvest: The Hijacking of the Global Food Supply*, South End Press.

69 'Protesters around the World March Against Monsanto,' *USA Today*, 26 May 2013.

70 For more information on the Save our Seeds (SOS) campaign, see www. saveourseeds.org/en.html.

71 For the full text of the Agreement, see 'WT/MIN(01)/DEC/2,' 20 November 2001, Declaration on the TRIPS Agreement and Public Health.

72 Novartis AG v. Union of India, Supreme Court of India. See en.wikipedia.org/wiki/Novartis_v._Union_of_India_%26_Others. See also Carlos Correa, 'Indian Court decision on Novartis Good Outcome for Public Health,' South Centre News, 11 November 2013.

73 The prime example of this is the IMF Institute for Capacity Development based in Washington, DC, with several regional centers. The institute produces technical and analytical papers on various aspects of development—all aimed at promoting the ideology of a free market economy. This ideology permeates the mainstream university teaching of economics, not only in the West but also in the countries of the South.

74 For further elaboration and discussion of the concept of imperialism, see chapter six.

75 On the concept of 'decoupling,' see chapter six.

76 Ramphal told this to me in 2001 when I accidentally ran into him at the WTO Doha conference. He was later to confirm this in an interview with the BBC. See Martin Plaut, 'Africa: US backed Zimbabwe land reform,' BBC News, 22 August 2007.

77 See http://mg.co.za/article/2013-11-28-mbeki-blair-plotted-military-intervention-in-zim.

78 On 17 April 1961, 1400 Cuban exiles—aided by the US—launched what became a botched invasion of Cuba at the Bay of Pigs. The attack was repulsed. In response to this invasion, Cuba requested that the USSR place nuclear missiles in Cuba to deter future US invasions. The USSR acceded to the request. This resulted in a direct confrontation between the US and the USSR at the height of the Cold War, leading to a thirteen-day standoff in October 1962. The USSR, fearing nuclear war, withdrew the missiles, and the US agreed not to invade Cuba in the future.

79 I have used various sources for collecting information on US sanctions on Cuba. I found Wikipedia's coverage of the subject very informative: http://en.wikipedia.org/wiki/United_States_embargo_against_Cuba.

80 Gary Hart, 'Fiction in Foreign Policy,' *Huffington Post*, 7 March 2011.

81 81. As we go to press, Cuba and the US have resumed 'normalization' of diplomatic relations. However, speaking at the Third Summit of the Community of Latin American and the Caribbean (CELAC) in January 28, 2015, President Raul Castro said that 'normalization' was 'not possible' unless the US respected the 'sovereign equality and reciprocity' in their relations, and ended the blockade as well as the 'illegal occupation' of Guantanamo (http://en.granma.cu/mundo/2015-01-29/president-raul-castro-speaks-to-third-celac-summit-in-costa-rica). His brother, Fidel, said that, while he welcomed the thawing of relations, 'I don't trust the policy of the United States' (http://www.dailymail.co.uk/news/article-2927784/Fidel-Castro-endorses-new-phase-Cuba-relations-statement-quashes-rumors-discord-brother-Raul.html#ixzz3RdrPDzmQ).'

82 All this information is as of August 2014. Things could change over time, though this seems unlikely in the foreseeable future.

83 See Alexander Brexendorff and Christian Ule, 'Changes bring new attention to Iranian buyback contracts,' Oil & Gas Journal, 1 November 2004.

84 See Platform IPS, War on Want, Global Policy Forum, Oil Change, NEF (2005), *Crude Designs: The rip-off of Iraq's oil wealth*,' Platform. (Download available from www.platformlondon.org.)

85 See Tim Kelly, 'Paul Krugman and Military Keynesianism,' 30 August 30 2011, http://fff.org/explore-freedom/articlse/paul-krugman-military-keynesianism.

86 The classic work in this area is Hans J. Morgenthau, *Politics Among Nations: The Struggle for Power and Peace*, 1967. Other key authors include E.H. Carr, Henry Kissinger, George Kennan and Samuel Huntington.

87 The so-called 'Underdevelopment' school of thought had its origins among Latin American scholars in the 1970s, and had considerable impact on African and Caribbean scholars such as Samir Amin and Walter Rodney. After the assault of neoliberal economics, the 'school' went into decline, but has in recent years picked up again.

88 The GCA was created around 1993, a brainchild of former World Bank President Robert McNamara. Its objective was 'to ensure that Africa remains high on the international agenda, to facilitate greater understanding of the development challenges faced by the continent, and to promote agreement on necessary actions to be taken by both African governments and their international partners. The GCA's agenda is focused on the broad themes of a) peace and security; b) governance and transition to democracy; and c) sustainable growth and integration into the global economy.' See http://web.worldbank.org/Website/External/Countries/Africaext/0. Nothing much is heard of the GCA anymore; it was simply a 'figment of the imagination' of Western imperialists like the World Bank that they could 'do the development' on behalf of Africa.

89 In 1983 the United Nations set up the World Commission on Environment and Development, headed by Gro Harlem Brundtland, the former Prime Minister of Norway. The Commission is also known as the Brundtland Commission.

90 First published in mid-1917 in pamphlet form in Petrograd. See Lenin (1963), *Lenin's Selected Works,* Vol. 1, Progress Publishers, pp. 667–766. I should add that Lenin's pamphlet was not entirely an original work. Lenin acknowledged his debt to, among others, J.A. Hobson's *Imperialism: A Study* (1902).

91 For an application of this analysis to the United States, see Perry Anderson, *American Foreign Policy and its Thinkers*, New Left Review, September/October, 2013.

92 Kwame Nkrumah (1966), *Neo-Colonialism: The Last Stage of Imperialism*, International Publishers, p. ix.

93 See Patrick Bond, 'BRICS and the tendency to sub-imperialism,' *Pambazuka News* 673, April 2014; Michael Abbott, *Sub imperialism the U.S. and*

Brazil in Morales' Bolivia; and Elif Çagli, *On Sub-imperialism Regional Power Turkey*, 2009.

94 For a further elaboration of this, see my 'On sub-imperialism and BRICS-bashing,' *Pambazuka News*, http://pambazuka.org/en/category/features/91832.

95 Of course, empires existed in the past. But those empires—such as the Chinese, Aztec, Greek, Roman and Ottoman—had their own characteristics. Here we are looking at imperialism in our own epoch, the capitalist epoch.

96 Abdul Sheriff (2010), *Dhow Cultures and the Indian Ocean: Cosmopolitanism, Commerce and Islam*, OUP.

97 See Terisa Turner (ed.), *Oil and Class Struggle*, Zed Press (with Peter Nore).

98 See R. Soares de Oliveira (2007), *Oil and Politics in the Gulf of Guinea*, Hurst.

99 See chapter three for background on the ACP and the Cotonou Agreement

100 'Somalia joins Cotonou Agreement,' *Sabahi*, 9 June 2013; and 'Mohamud praises Somalia's membership in Cotonou Agreement,' *Sabahi*, 10 June 2013.

101 Shawn Helton, '*The Horns of Africa: Neo-Colonialism, Oil Wars and Terror Games*,' www.globalresearch.ca/the-horns-of-africa-neo-colonialism-oil-wars-and-terror-games/5355993.

102 See www.rigzone.com/news/oil_gas/a/133442/Soma_Oil_Gas_Completes_Seismic_Acquisition_Program_Offshore_Somalia.

103 See http://finance.yahoo.com/news/hank-paulson-warns-another-financial-171148084.html.

104 Both Fukuyama and Huntington come from mainstream Western geopolitical and ideological thinking, based essentially on Eurocentric epistemologies. They boil down, in the case of Fukuyama, to a premature celebration of Western triumphalism at the end of the Cold War and the demise of the Soviet Union, and in the case of Huntington, to a fear of counter-Western civilisations, especially Islamic ones. See Francis Fukuyama (1992), *The End of History and the Last Man*, Free Press; and Samuel P. Huntington (1996), *The Clash of Civilizations and the Remaking of World Order*, Simon and Schuster.

105 It is usual to contrast 'civilization' to supposedly barbarian or primitive cultures, such as those of hunter-gatherers and nomadic pastoralists. The word 'primitive' is highly pejorative and demeans many cultures—such as the Karamojong of Uganda, among whom I grew up as a child—that

in many ways have a higher culture (in the sense of social bonding and peaceful means of internal conflict resolution) than our 'modern' industrial or post-industrial civilisations.

106 At the time of writing these lines, there was a Scottish referendum (19 September 2014) on whether Scotland should separate from England as a 'nation.' A clear majority voted against independence, but it is unlikely that the process will wither away.

107 Enlightenment thinkers like Edward Gibbon, the author of the classic *The Decline and Fall of the Roman Empire*, and even the writings of the English historian Arnold Toynbee, had a very balanced view of Islam. These and many historians have written that after the Prophet's death in AD 632, Islam spread to all surrounding areas, bringing lands from Persia to Spain under its control. From the seventh century to about the beginning of the Crusades—for some five hundred years—Islam was not only a formidable force but culturally, scientifically and intellectually progressive. The Caliphates encouraged merchants and scholars to travel through Western Eurasia, bringing goods and knowledge to Europe. In 751, for example, paper-making from China made its way to Europe through Muslim traders. Future states of the region, such as the Safavid, Seljuk, Ottoman and Mughal in India, were all Islamic.

108 The Crusaders adopted the conquered area's gold bezant coins with Arabic legends.

109 For a fascinating account of this, see Stephen Zarlenga (2002), *The Lost Science of Money*, American Monetary Institute Charitable Trust.

110 ISIS is a self-proclaimed 'state' that has sought to establish its authority in the region of the Levant, including Syria, Jordan, Lebanon, Israel, Palestine, and southern Turkey.

111 '*Why Young Europeans Join ISIS?*' Charlotte Van Hek–October 4, 2014. http://euron.co.uk/why-young-europeans-join-isis/

112 See Patrick Cockburn (2014), *The Jihadis Return*, OR Books, p. 9.

113 See https://sustainablecrediton.org.uk/economics/reading/christine-lagarde.aspx. Because Lagarde talks from an institutional perspective, my criticism is not personal but institutional.

114 See http://www.nbcnews.com/storyline/military-spending-cuts/u-s-military-spending-dwarfs-rest-world-n37461.

115 The 'productive forces' include science and technology, which have grown astronomically over the last hundred years, and the organisa-

tion of the production of commodities. Marx posited the term 'relations of production' to represent the social infrastructure of production, including people's relationships, ideology and culture. It is, Marx said, the combination of the productive forces and the relations of production that constitute a historically specific 'mode of production.' I use these terms because they are useful analytical categories, but I do not wish to get into a discourse on this.

116 See http://www.oecd.org/social/soc/dividedWestandwhyinequalitykeep-srising.htm.

117 See the excellent series brought out (in 2013–14) by *Centre Europe-Tiers Monde* (CETIM) on some of the African leaders of the past—among them Frantz Fanon, Amilcar Cabral, Mehdi Ben Barka, Patrice Lumumba, Thomas Senkara, and Julius Nyerere.

118 To reduce these to science and technology and the organisation of production of material goods would be rather simplistic, but it captures the essence of the concept.

119 See also Samir Amin (2011), *Ending the Crisis of Capitalism or Ending Capitalism?*, Pambazuka Press.

120 See http://opinionator.blogs.nytimes.com/2014/03/15/on-the-wrong-side-of-globalization/?_php=true&_type=blogs&_php=true&_type=blogs&ref=josephestiglitz&_r=1.

121 In 2009 the United Nations General Assembly set up a commission under Stiglitz to undertake an analysis of the economic and financial crisis and make recommendations. The commission's report carried out a fairly good analysis. It made a set of ten recommendations which were more or less along the lines of Christine Laggard's above-mentioned reformist suggestions, though with more detail and backed by evidence and a concrete plan of action. However, none of its ten recommendations (five years down the line) has been implemented. That shows that the 'international community' is not ready to change the global financial infrastructure at the top. The IMF and the World Bank are unreformable in the present geopolitical context. One consequence of this is that there are active efforts to create parallel structures, such as the BRICS-initiated Development Bank, which is still in its early days.

122 See also Yilmaz Akyuz, 'Are Developing Countries Waving or Drowning?' *South Bulletin* #76, 21 November 2013. He says: 'After 2009 several

Developing Countries started to control capital inflows, mainly through market-friendly measures rather than direct restrictions. These included unremunerated reserve requirements (URR) and taxes (Brazil taxes on portfolio inflows; Peru on foreign purchases of CB [Central Bank] paper; and Colombia URR of 40 per cent for 6 months); minimum stay or holding periods (Colombia for inward FDI; Indonesia for CB papers); special reserve requirements (RR) and taxes on banks' positions (Brazil RR on short positions and tax on short positions in forex derivatives; Indonesia RR for total foreign assets; Peru higher RR on non-resident local currency deposits); taxes and restrictions over borrowing abroad (India on corporate borrowing; Indonesia on bank borrowing; Peru additional capital requirements for forex credit exposure); and taxes on foreign earnings on financial assets (Thailand withholding tax on interest income and capital gains from domestic bonds). Some DCs such as South Africa liberalised outflows by residents in order to relieve the upward pressure on the currency.'

123 Another decoupled innovation in the finance sector is Bitcoin. Bitcoin is a crypto-currency that uses peer-to-peer technology to operate with no central authority or bank. Nobody owns or controls Bitcoin. See http://bitcoin.org/en.

124 Karl Mannheim (1954), *Ideology and Utopia: An Introduction to the Sociology of Knowledge*, Harcourt Brace.

125 Nassim Taleb, 2007, *The Black Swan: the Impact of the Highly Improbable,* Penguin Books.

126 Dani Nabudere (2011), *Afrikology: Philosophy and Wholeness: An Epistemology*, and (2012) *Afrikology and Transdisciplinarity: A Restorative Epistemology,* published by the African Institute of South Africa, in its 'Development through Knowledge' series.

127 See Yash Tandon, '*Pitfalls of Humanitarian Interventionism—Responsibility to Protect (R2p): A Perspective from Africa,*' paper presented at the Doshisha University International Conference on Asian Perspectives on Humanitarian Interventions in the 21st Century, Kyoto, 28–29 June 2011, http://global-studies.doshisha.ac.jp/attach/page/GLOBAL_STUDIES-PAGE-JA-24/24946/file/asia-program.pdf.

128 Sun Tzu (1991), *The Art of War*, translated by Thomas Cleary, Shambala Pocket Classic.

129 Ibid, p. 90.

FURTHER READING

Amin, Samir (2011), *Ending the Crisis of Capitalism or Ending Capitalism?*, Pambazuka Press

Chomsky, Noam (1993), *Year 501—The Conquest Continues*, New York, Black Rose Books.

Fanon, Frantz (1952), *Black Skin, White Masks* (1967) translation by Charles Lam Markmann, New York: Grove Press

Gardner, R.N. (1956) *Sterling-Dollar Diplomacy*, New York: Clarendon Press.

Gibbon, Edward (1909–1914) *The Decline and Fall of the Roman Empire*, 6 Volumes, Kindle edition, 2014

Hudec, Robert E. (1999), *Essays on the Nature of International Trade Law*, Cameron.

Hudson, Michael (1992), *Trade, Development and Foreign Trade*, in two volumes, London: Pluto Press

Huntington, S. (1996), *The Clash of Civilizations and the Remaking of World Order*, Simon and Schuster

Lenin, V.I. (1916) *Imperialism, the Highest Stage of Capitalism*, Lenin Internet Archive 2005.

Morgenthau, Hans J. (1967), *Politics Among Nations: The Struggle for Power and Peace*, New York, Knopf

Nabudere, Dani W. (2011) *Afrikology: Philosophy and Wholeness: An Epistemology*, African Institute of South Africa

Nkrumah, Kwame. (1966), *Neo-Colonialism: The Last Stage of Imperialism*, International Publishers

Reinert, Erik S. (2007) *How Rich Countries Got Rich . . . and Why Poor Countries Stay Poor*, London: Constable.

Shiva, Vandana, (2000), *Stolen Harvest: The Hijacking of the Global Food Supply*, South End Press.

Skidelsky, Robert (2000). *John Maynard Keynes, Vol. 3: Fighting for Britain, 1937–1946*, McMillan.

Soros, George (2004), *The Bubble of American Supremacy—Correcting the Misuse of American Power*, London: Weidenfeld & Nicolson

Sumner, Andy and Meera Tiwari (2009). *After 2015: International Development Policy at a Crossroads*, Palgrave.

Susan, George (1976), *How the Other Half Dies: The Real Reasons for World Hunger*, Penguin

Taleb, Nassim (2007), *The Black Swan: the Impact of the Highly Improbable*, Penguin Books

Tandon, Yash (2001). '*My Attempt to Enter the Boiler Room at Doha Ministerial*,' *SEATINI Bulletin*, 30 November 2001

Tandon, Yash (2008). *Ending Aid Dependence*, Geneva: South Centre and UK: Fahamu Books

Tandon, Yash (2012). *Demystifying Aid*, Pambazuka Insights. Fahamu Books

Toynbee, Arnold, (1934–1961), *A Study of History*, Oxford University Press, 12 volumes

Tzu, Sun (1991), *The Art of War*, translated by Thomas Cleary, Shambala Pocket Classic.

Ziegler, Jean, 2011. *The Fight for the Right to Food: Lessons Learnt*, Palgrave

GLOSSARY

Acephalous international system: An absence of a centralised global governance structure

Asymmetric war: war between the North and the South whether on actual battlefield or in the trade arena

Chimurenga: Wars People of Zimbabwe have been fighting against British colonial conquest and continuing control

Cognitive Reframing: Reframing one's perspective about events and their analysis. For example, World War I and II from an Arab perspective

Critical or Revolutionary Realism: Recognising the existential Reality whilst transforming it fundamentally

Decoupling-Delinking: Distancing ones nation and economy from the command and control system of globalisation Development aid.

Dependency or Underdevelopment Theory: that free trade 'underdevelops' the 'periphery' of Southern states to the advantage of the wealthy Western 'core' states

Dynamic forces and Revolutionary forces: Forces generated by exploited sections of society and by science and technology that transform the relations of production (see relations of production)

Eurocentric epistemology and pedagogy: the myth that the West is the source of all knowledge

'Evergreening' technology: the process by which drug companies maintain artificially high prices on medicines by continually extending patent protection for 'minor modifications' to existing drugs

Exchange and use values: exchange value refers to an item or service produced and traded as a commodity for a price; use value refers to its consumption whether or not traded as a commodity.

Genocide: killing of large numbers of people, usually of a particular nation, ethnic group, or religion

Ideology: a structured set of ideas and values that forms the basis of philosophical, economic, and political worldview

Imperial Peace: Western/NATO defined democracy, globalisation and militarism

Imperialism: is specific to each historical epoch. In the Capitalist era it takes the form of colonisation, export of capital, occupation and control over the colonised people and their resources

Intifada: is coined by the people of Palestine. In this book, generally, it means resistance or struggle against imperialism

Kohwa Pakuru: literally, 'reap big' or 'increased harvest' promoted by Ciba Gigy (Noartis) in Zimbabwe

Labour vouchers: Unlike money, these are based on labour-time spent on providing a consumable item or service (see also exchange and use values)

Mhondoro: 'royal ancestors' (Zimbabwe)

Money: The medium of settling debt or storing savings in a particular historical context.

Nakbah: catastrophe. It refers to the forced expulsion of Palestinians from their homeland by Israel in 1947

Neo-Colonialism: Post-colonial imperialism (see Imperialism)

Neo-liberal ideology: A set of economic policies based on the myth of free market and pushed by the Western imperial nations since the mid-1980s

Nganga: is a Bantu term for an herbalist or spiritual healer in many African societies and also in many societies of the African diaspora, such as those in Brazil.

Occidentalism: is a set of cultures and values of the West viewed from the perspective of the South (see Orientalism)

Orientalism: is a set of cultures and values of the South (the Orient) viewed from the perspective of the West

Paradigm and Paradigm Shift: Following Kuhn, a paradigm is the total knowledge system and worldview of a historical period; a paradigm shift occurs when that knowledge system is challenged

Precautionary principle: The principle that if there is a risk that an action or policy might cause harm to the public or to the environment, then, in the absence of scientific evidence, it is prudent to exercise caution.

Primitive accumulation: the pre-Capitalist accumulation of capital, usually done through force and dispossession or colonisation

Relations of Production: the relationship between those who own or control the means of production (such as land and capital) and those who do not

Solidarity: unity with a group of nations or people based on shared values and interests and without exploitation

Systemic causality: is based on a total or holistic, as opposed to fragmented, view of the cause of a phenomenon

Utupa (Trifosea Vogelli), albida, and *nzigati*: trees used in Tanzania for soil conservation

INDEX

YASH TANDON is the author of numerous books and is an Honorary Professor at Warwick and London Middlesex Universities in the UK. He is the Founder-Chairman of SEATINI (Southern and Eastern African Trade Information and Negotiations Institute), and former Executive Director of the South Centre, a think tank of the Global South.